MW00454127

SKETCHES OF GOD

SKETCHES OF GOD

Carlos G. Valles, S.J.

1987
GUJARAT SAHITYA PRAKASH
ANAND—388 001
INDIA

American printing produced in 1987 and distributed by Loyola
University Press, 3441 North Ashland Avenue, Chicago, Illinois 60657,
with permission of the publisher.

CONTENTS

Images, I must suppose, have their use, or they would not have been so popular. (It makes little difference whether they are pictures and statues outside the mind or imaginative constructions within it.) To me, however, their danger is more obvious. Images of the Holy easily become holy images — sacrosanct. My idea of God is not a divine idea. It has to be shattered time after time. He shatters it Himself. He is the great iconoclast. Could we not almost say that this shattering is one of the marks of His presence? The Incarnation is the supreme example; it leaves all previous ideas of the Messiah in ruins. And most are 'offended' by the iconoclasm; and blessed are those who are not.

C. S. Lewis

TELL ME YOUR GOD...

I have often been asked in my life: "What has India given you?" And the final answer I give is: "India has enlarged and enriched the concept I had of God..., and that is possibly the best service she has rendered me."

Such is the final answer I give, and by that I mean that it has taken me a long long time to reach the clarity and finality of that little formula. I have lived in India for almost forty years, and at the beginning, apart from the fact that nobody then asked me the question, I would not have thought of giving such an answer. For one thing, it required a good deal of reflection and maturity which only time could supply, and, for another, my attitude when coming to India was not precisely to "receive", but to "give"; I was arrogant enough to think that I was coming to teach, not to learn; it was I who was going to do "something" for India, not India for me. I did not know then that learning, if it is to take place at all, must be mutual, that true teaching is always a two-way traffic, that in order to give I must open my mind and my ideas; and that once the hand and the heart and the mind have thus been opened, they become ready to receive, to take in,

1

to be enriched in their turn by the environment they had come to enrich. In a perfectly oriental paradox (and we may begin already to learn from the Orient, home and climate of the paradox) to give is to receive, and to teach is to learn.

When the question "What has India given you?" began to turn up in conversations with friends and interviews with newsmen, my first answers were, however true and honest, unavoidably superficial. India has given me friendship, and that is true because my best friends are Indians. But then I also imagine that my best friends would be Japanese if I had lived forty years in Japan. India has given me success in academic and literary fields with a generosity that already exceeds merit, and would have been difficult to match in other more critical and exacting climates. This is also part of that great virtue, that generous quality which is largely Oriental and specifically Indian, and of which the West is simply ignorant, the virtue of total hospitality of board and of thought, of a door always open for the unannounced guest, and a mind always ready for the unexpected idea. I have used and abused that blessed hospitality, both the culinary and the philosphical, from house to house and from audience to audience, and it has given me a precious and intimate gift, the gift of belonging, of feeling at home, of being accepted, of having a few families which I consider as my own, and many that consider me as their own; and with that the right to speak, feel and write on Indian culture from the inside, without having to ask permission or give explanations, free to rejoice, to accept, to dissent and to see the world in a different way without censorship and without fear. Hearty welcome to a new way of life.

From that experience came new answers to the repeated question. What has India given you? Broad-mindedness, an enlarged vision, a linguistic treat, practical

2

methods of unusual contemplation, ecumenism in the streets, and living contact with multiple philosophies and popular mysticism. As I was getting to know India better and to know myself better, a new answer was taking shape within me without my realizing it, an answer that was to sum up all the other answers and set them aside once and for all, or rather to take them up as fragments that were to fit together and achieve full sense in the final revelation.

The revelation came, full-grown and decisive, on a particular occasion I remember well. Ishwar Petlikar, dear friend and admired colleague in the business of writing, was one day asking me questions, paper and pencil in hand, with a view to an article in the monthly magazine of which he was the editor, when, towards the end of the interview he said, still holding the pencil at the ready for a last punch line in his planned article: "You have given much to India in the many years you have been here, your work, your life, your books that have done much good to many; and now I ask you with parallel curiosity: What has India in turn given you in your life?" And it was there, in the warmth of the exchange and the sincerity of our friendship, that the answer came out straight and full-grown. "India", I blurted out, "has enlarged the concept I had of God, and that is her greatest favour to me ever." Petlikar, shrewd editor that he was after all, kept his pencil poised over the paper in momentary suspense, and looked up at me with a quizzical smile as if to say: "Are you not bluffing me just now? Are you not getting off at a tangent? Are you not giving me only a pious answer, a devout cliché, when what I want is a bold and catchy answer for the readers of my magazine? Come on now, get off it soon and give me something more concrete and spicy which my pencil may take down and my readers may read!" We knew and loved each other too well for cheating. I

3

understood his look, and explained my answer. I explain it now here.

My behaviour is determined by my beliefs, and my beliefs are ruled by the supreme belief that is faith in God. The concept I have of God is what, in the last analysis, presides over my life and shapes my convictions. One has only to look at the Homeric gods to understand Greek character in the time of Homer, and a study of the mythology of the African jungle is essential to understand the behaviour of its tribes. Tell me your God, and I will tell you your life. This holds, not only from one religion to another, but within the same creed and the same baptism. Tell me how you conceive God, how you address him, how you pray to him, how you imagine him when you talk to him, how you interpret his commandments and how you react when you break them; tell me what it is that you expect from him in this life and in the next, what you have learned about him and read about him, tell me what you know about him and you believe about him..., tell me all that, and you will have told me the whole biography of your own soul. The concept a person has of God is the summary of his own life.

And that concept, in me, would have been much poorer and colourless if I had not come to India. Here is where my own personal theology changed in the heat of the tropics, my idea of God opened up to new features and new revelations, and with that my whole life too broke open, my horizon broadened, and my thought and my behaviour took new flight. Both history and geography have made India into an intrinsically ecumenical land. In India live, side by side, ways of understanding God as different as Vedantic monism and tribal animism, in India are accepted and practised almost all the great religions of the world, and what is

4

more, they are found face to face and heart to heart in persons one meets daily, in simple conversation and in deep friendship. Here ideas have a face, and the different religions bear the names of friends and acquaintances. That is the deep and generous blessing of this sacred land where the heat and rain of the monsoon (which quite unexpectedly will have an important role to play at a key moment in this story) nurse religious thought as a favourite crop in its open fields.

I regret that Ishwar Petlikar will not read these pages. I would have enjoyed going through them with him, discussing together the thoughts he shook into expression with a timely question. Both he is no longer here. He had asked me to preside over the celebrations that his friends and admirers had lovingly planned for him on his sixtieth birthday. I felt honoured at the invitation and accepted it with joy; I only put one condition, half serious half in jest, that he would preside over my celebrations when I reached sixty. We sealed the pact, and I carried out my part of it; but he could not carry out his. One day, out on the open highway, he bade the car stop. He sensed his heart was failing him. All the hospitals around opened their doors to him; all knew the popular writer, and they were able to fend off the first attack. But a relapse a few days later took him away. When we, his friends, got together to relive our mutual memories in posthumous tribute, I mentioned his gift of the pointed question which liberated the answer tied up within me, and which, for ever now, will be linked with him in my memory. India has enlarged my concept of God, and that is the greatest service it could have rendered me.

There is more to this than a purely personal experience or a piece of intimate biography. The religious crisis we are living today is a crisis of values, of credibility, faith, institu-

5

tions, of the meaning of life and the burden of man's suffering, and, therefore, a crisis bearing on the concept of God which underlies them all and shows through them all, giving different shapes to the one basic and vital uneasiness. Who and what is God, the God who asks for those values, those institutions, those regulations, those sufferings? A whole generation of believers has learned and lives on a concrete concept of God, legitimate but limited, as all human concepts of God are limited. It finds itself, by training or character, unable or unwilling to enlarge its catechism or contemplate alternative understandings, and, as a consequence, when they meet situations in life that do not fit in with that concept, they reject the concept and reject God. That is, they reject the God they imperfectly knew. If they had known him better, they would not have left him. That is why we have to enlarge the understanding, open windows in the mind, liberate concepts and welcome renovations. We have to let God be God.

The best way to fight atheism (mission of missions in today's world as it has always been) is to obtain a better understanding of God. That, and no less, is the quixotic ambition of this book.

THE FIRST LOVE

"I saw you blissfully smiling towards the tabernacle in the chapel", said a devotional friend to me when we both were young and innocent. I blushed. It was true that I had done so, and to see my piety uncovered made my cheeks go red. Not that I was ashamed, on the contrary, I felt happy at heart to have a friendly witness of my intimacy with Jesus; but the very intensity of the love I felt surged up and warmed my face when it heard itself expressed in words of one who understood the feeling because he shared in the romance. Yes, I had gone to the chapel, had "spoken" with Jesus, had enjoyed his company so much that the inner joy had showed itself, and the bliss of my heart became a smile on my lips. And someone saw it and came and told me. Blessed simplicity of life's first love.

The discovery of Jesus as a person in my adolescence, the warmth of his friendship, the reality of his presence, the majesty of his divinity and the sheer charm of his earthly manner made up a solid and immense reality that has been the basis and foundation of all that has come afterwards in my life. It may have been a naive attitude, elementary,

7

precritical, anthropomorphic; but the strength and the light that the feeling of a personal friendship with Jesus brought to the fervent years of my happy youth was such an intense and real experience that without it I would not be able to understand my own life—whatever the multiple vicissitudes it has passed through since. In fact (and with this I am already pointing at future conflicts) that relationship was so intensely blissful that it would later be hard for me to detach myself from it, as the Magdalene from the feet of Jesus on Easter morning, in order to transcend transitory contacts in search of a new resurrected presence.

I remember my first copy of the Gospels, personal treasure of almost physical joy in greedy possession. I bought it with my own pocket money, I would caress it, kiss it, place it tenderly under my pillow when I went to bed with the almost ridiculous gesture of a romantic lover; but the fact is that I missed it if I did not have it bodily with me. In that atmosphere came for me the first complete and continuous reading of the inspired texts of the four evangelists. Many passages where already known and familiar to me, but then suddenly an entirely new paragraph emerged, a sentence of Jesus I had never heard, an episode which, as it did not figure in the shy liturgy of those restricted days, was brand-new to me, and its first reading took up a sacred air of surprise, revelation, secret initiation and intimate joy that consecrated the new words with sacramental faith. At times I would run up to a friend to tell him the latest news with bursting enthusiasm: "Did you know that Jesus had said this?" "I bet you had never read this sentence in the Gospel!" "See what a wonderful passage I've discovered today!" The friendship with Jesus born straight from the pages of the Gospels was so great and so new that it had to be shared with others; only so could my own soul bear its glorious burden.

8

An anecdote of Father Rubio, which I read about that time, describes my world in those happy days. Good Father Rubio (now on his way to the altars) was going to board a train or a bus, and when asking for the ticket said absent-mindedly, "Two tickets for..., please." Then suddenly he checked himself and said apologetically with a touch of pleasant embarrassment: "Sorry, not two tickets, only one if you don't mind." The presence by his side of the eternal Friend was so real for him that while taking a ticket for himself he spontaneously thought he had to take another ticket for Jesus. How could he allow him to pay for himself, or, worse, to travel without a ticket? His faith was so real that it almost made him pay double for his trip. That was the ideal, and, at some privileged moments, the living experience of my own youth. Jesus, my friend, always by my side.

Lacordaire had been preaching for ten years from the exclusive pulpit of Notre Dame in Paris, and was then at the peak of his fame as the greatest preacher of the day. He had spoken of morals and apologetics, of the family and of society, of faith and of the Church, and finally in 1846 he brought himself to speak directly about the person of Jesus to that distinguished audience. At that moment he set aside the rather academic tone that had characterized his conferences till then, he addressed himself directly to Jesus, and broke into a lyrical colloquy which I then learned by heart without effort, and can still recite today: "Lord Jesus, it is now ten years that I have been speaking to this audience about your Church. True, it is about you after all that I was speaking all this time; but finally today I have come more directly to your own person. Today I have come to yourself, to that divine figure that is every day the object of my contemplation; to your sacred feet which I have kissed so many times; to your loving hands which have blessed me so often; to your head

9

crowned with glory and with thorns; to that life whose perfume I breathed since my birth; to that life which I rejected in
my adolescence; which I found back again in my youth; and
which now in my manhood I adore and announce to every
creature. O father! O master! O friend! O Jesus! Help me now
more than ever before; that my audience may realize that
now I am closer to you; and that the words that come from
my lips may tell them that you are closer to me."

Even closer to my heart were the words of Teresa of
Avila with the candid realism of her irresistible experience.
She too, in her autobiography, goes on describing situations
and happenings in her life, when suddenly she can hold
herself back no more, lets go of her narrative and addresses
Jesus directly on the written page to unburden herself before
him in the impossibility of telling others all that he is. Unfortunately no translation can even remotely reproduce the impulsive charm of her live prose. Here is an attempt. "O King
of glory and Lord of all kings! Yours is not a plaster kingdom
that crumbles at the touch, but one that has no end. And
yours is a royalty that needs no retinue. To look at you is
enough to have to call you Lord. You need no escort to
make all realize that you are king. Down here a king, if he
goes all alone by himself, will not be recognized as a king, as
he will look just like any other person. He needs his court
and his horses and his trumpets and his throne; he needs
the make up and the peruke of a king to appear like one, he
gets his look of authority from his dress and from his en-
tourage. That is a borrowed look that has no substance. O
my Lord! O my King! Who could now describe the majesty
that you bring with your very presence! It is impossible to fail
to realize that you are supreme Emperor in yourself. Your
majesty asserts itself on its own. And even more so your
humility in deigning to show love to one like me."

10

The surprise of an old Latin verse tucked away like a sparkling jewel in the severe folds of the official breviary, sums up with pointed feeling the overwhelming happiness of the direct love to him who deserves it most and repays it best: *"Quem vidi, quem amavi; in quem credidi, quem dilexi."* "I saw him, I loved him; I put my faith in him, I put all my love in him." That is the bare and basic experience of the encounter with God, all the more genuine in its reality as the fewer words are needed for its expression. The concise formula contains already in germ and promise all that is to follow by way of thought, reflection, theology, prayer, doubts, crises, synthesis and silence. All that will happen and be welcome and will fill up books and make up a life. But all of it was genetically contained in the initial experience of youthful love with the friend who was God. The innocent smile before the beloved tabernacle in the chapel.

KING OF KINGS

Familiarity with God in Jesus is a sublime gift that justifies a life. And, precisely because it is an exalted privilege, it is of necessity beset with dangers and excesses. In human relations experience has framed the saying "familiarity breeds contempt", and, without reaching such an extreme in our relationship with God, excessive familiarity makes us forget the other and equally essential pole of God's nature; that is his transcendence, the distant remoteness of the "Wholly Other", the depth of a mystery we can never fathom, the burning bush that has to be approached without sandals, the cloud, the night, the mountain and the tempest. All that is God too, and we cannot afford to forget it.

Tradition links the name of the beloved disciple, John, with the last Gospel, and with the last book of the Bible, the book of Revelation. Both the books come, if not literally from his pen, certainly from his school, from his disciples, from his teaching. The fourth Gospel, intensely aware on each page that Jesus is the Christ, the Son of God, and consequently zealous guardian and herald of his divinity,

13

presents all the same with bold intimacy the human traits of Jesus' personality, and speaks of personal contacts with him, of long conversations at night in solitude, of favoured friendship, confidences, affection and tenderness that bring God closer to the heart of man than any other book in the Bible. John has always been the favourite Gospel for those who wanted to draw close to the God-with-us who was announced in the Old Testament and became a reality in the New. From the first call in the Joannine pages, "Come and see", so that "they went and saw where he was staying, and spent the rest of the day with him", to the moment when man reclines his head on God's own breast in bold gesture and loving invitation during a night of farewells; from the Samaritan woman at the well to the Magdalene at the empty tomb, God comes closer to men and women on earth than any prophet could have foreseen or any religion could have dreamt. "I will no longer call you servants but friends." The seal of intimacy, final and definitive proof that God has become man, is firmly imprinted on the pages that are the charter of our revelation, and with it the definition of our creed and of our life.

And now the pages of the other "Revelation" in name and in reality, the book that closes the Bible, and which we also call "Apocalypse" (that is again Greek for "revelation"). "I turned to see whose voice it was that spoke to me; and when I turned I saw seven standing lamps of gold, and among the lamps one like a Son of Man, robed down to his feet, with a golden girdle round his breast. The hair of his head was white as snow-white wool, and his eyes flamed like fire; his feet gleamed like burnished brass refined in a furnace, and his voice was like the sound of rushing waters. In his right hand he held seven stars, and out of his mouth came a sharp two-edged sword; and his face shone like the sun in full strength. When I saw him, I fell at his feet as though dead. But he laid his right hand upon me and said, 'Do not be afraid. I am the first and the last, and I am the living one; for I was dead and now I am alive for evermore, and I hold the keys of Death and Death's domain.' " (1:12-18).

Another passage: "Then I saw heaven wide open, and there before me was a white horse; and its rider's name was Faithful and True, for he is just in judgement and just in war. His eyes flamed like fire, and on his head were many diadems. Written upon him was a name known to none but himself, and he was robed in a garment drenched in blood. He was called the Word of God, and the armies of heaven followed him on white horses, clothed in fine linen, clean and shining. From his mouth there went a sharp sword with which to smite the nations; for he it is who shall rule them with an iron rod, and tread the winepress of the wrath and retribution of God the sovereign Lord. And on his robe and on his thigh there was written the name: King of kings and Lord of lords." (19:11-16).

No wonder that on seeing these visions the seer should fall at his feet like one dead, rather than lean on his breast as a beloved companion. Jesus is the same, but now the majesty tempers the closeness, and the power allays the familiarity. King of kings and Lord of lords. The experience of one disciple embraces both extremes, both visions, both theologies, the one close by and the one far away, because they complement each other, and both are needed for the fullness of the truth.

The paradox of the book of Revelation is that in the very process of revealing God it stresses his being beyond all knowledge, and while bringing us close to him, emphasizes the distance. When the seer is invited to the presence of the throne and comes to see "One seated on the throne" whom the twenty-four elders worship in permanent liturgy of gesture and song, he finds that "in front of it stretched what seemed a sea of glass, like a sheet of ice" (4:6), which later becomes "a sea of glass shot with fire" (15:2), on whose shore are standing those who have already obtained victory, holding harps on their hands, and singing the song that Moses had sung one day by the side of another sea through which too God had passed.

The sea is a cosmogonic symbol of all chaos and all beginnings, of depth and distance, of the origin of life and the watery grave of death. The sea keeps continents apart, breeds tempests and designs horizons. And it is beyond that primeval and eternal sea that the throne of God is placed, even for the official receptions in the court of the chosen ones. Sea of glass and fire, at one time transparent and incandescent, cold like frost and burning with flames, desert and iceberg, equator and Antarctica, lightning and hail. Jealous guardian of God's secret even before those who are admitted into his presence. Before the goal of the throne, the barrier of the sea.

Another parable of "Revelation". The white colour. White was the colour of Jesus' garment when, for an instant of glory in the midst of thirty-three years of submission, the splendour of his divinity shone on top of a mountain, and the eyes of the three chosen disciples were blinded with the light of his transfigured countenance. And in the book of Revelation white are the garments of the elect (3:5, 7:9), as those of the Bride (19:8); white is the horse on which the Word of God rides, and white is God's own throne (20:11). White is the colour of purity, of brightness, the union of all colours when they blend into one their seven separate identi-

16

ties; white is a colour difficult to protect from stain in the tur-
moil of dust and passions we stir up here below, and so it
becomes the natural symbol and evident image of that which
we cannot obtain or keep by ourselves, of all that is beyond
our doing and our understanding, of the throne of God and
of God himself who eternally sits on it in his inaccessible
purity and sanctity. The whiteness of God beyond the stained hands of man.

The book of Revelation is the ritual for the liturgy of
heaven, the book of ceremonies for eternity, the manual for
the court ceremonial in the company of the angels. We have
to practise here its rules before we join their ranks. And that
manual teaches us above all respect and reverence, distance
and awe, the bended knee and the bowed head, the total
and ultimate worship and adoration of the naked creature
before its Creator and Lord. To feel at home in heaven, we
have to train ourselves in reverence while here on earth.

"The four living creatures, each of them with six wings,
had eyes all over, inside and out; and by day and by night
without a pause they sang: Holy, holy, holy is God the
sovereign Lord of all, who was, and is, and is to come! As
often as the living creatures give glory and honour and
thanks to the One who sits on the throne, who lives for ever
and ever, the twenty-four elders fall down before the One
who sits on the throne and worship him who lives for ever
and ever; and as they lay their crowns before the throne
they cry: You are worthy, O Lord our God, to receive glory
and honour and power, because you created all things; by
your will they were created, and have their being." (4:8-11).

If we want to advance in the knowledge of God we cannot stop at the Gospels. We have to read the whole Bible till
the end.

17

THOU SHALT NOT MAKE IMAGES OF GOD

"You shall not make a carved image for yourself nor the likeness of anything in the heavens above, or on the earth below, or in the waters under the earth. You shall not bow to them or worship them." (Ex 20:4-5).

This commandment, which is the second in Moses' tablets, not only forbids images of other gods, of the false gods worshipped by Israel's neighbours and rivals, but, with greater depth and urgency, it proscribes and outlaws for ever images of Yahweh himself from the land of Israel. Israel is to be different from the other peoples that surround it, and so it has not to conceive a limited or partial God, it has not to be satisfied with a harvest god or a war god, with a finite and concrete god who can be painted or sculptured in stone to say once and for ever in marble and colour what that god is and what he can do. No. Israel will let God free to be whatever he is ("I am who I am") and to do whatever he pleases in any circumstance. Israel will not degrade the concept of God with the idolatry of the brush, nor imprison it in molten brass or in carved stone. Israel shall not have images of Yahweh. The temple, yes, will be decorated with figures

19

of "cherubim, palms and open flowers" (1 Kgs 6:32), but the cover of the Ark, between the two gold cherubim, "where I shall meet you" (Ex 25:22), will remain flat and plain, expressing the presence of God by the absence of any ornament. Israel accepted the commandment because it understood its meaning and realized its importance for the purity of its faith and the unity of its people.

It was Jeroboam who first broke the commandment, and caused in consequence the ruin of Israel. When Solomon died, Jeroboam, who had been exiled to Egypt for his subversive influence on the working classes, came back, rebelled against Rehoboam, Solomon's unpopular son, and the whole Israel followed him except the tribes of Benjamin and Judah in Jerusalem. Jeroboam enjoyed military superiority, but Rehoboam occupied Jerusalem, and with it the Temple, the only place of worship and therefore a constant attraction for every Israelite wherever he might be. Jeroboam feared that his own people, now in the Northern Kingdom, would abandon him in order to go and offer sacrifices in the Temple at Jerusalem, and so he decided to strengthen his military and political power with the religious power which was even more important. He had to break the monopoly of Jerusalem and its Temple. To achieve that he ordered two images of Yahweh to be made, and installed one in Bethel and the other in Dan; then he solemnly consecrated the images, established a regular priesthood, fixed the feast of the annual festival, and thus gave rise in Israel to the cult of a visible Yahweh, fashioned into the shape of a golden calf. And Israel's history followed its theology. The visible image brought in the scism, the split, the division of Israel, set in motion its decadence and caused its ruin. The sanctuary at Bethel became the rival of the Temple of Jerusalem. It was only after the exile that Israel became one again.

Jeroboam was remembered in Israel as the cause of its downfall, and whenever his name is mentioned in the sacred text, it goes accompanied by the scathing refrain, "Jeroboam, who taught Israel to sin". The sin was to make a visible image of Yahweh for the people to worship.

And now is the time to turn the spotlight on ourselves and to realize and acknowledge that we too, together with the majority of the Israelites at Solomon's death, are also followers of Jeroboam. We have voted for Dan and Bethel, we have manufactured golden calves, we have fashioned for ourselves images of God far more dangerous than gold and silver, because they are subtle images, mental images, scholastic definitions, prayerful titles which we use and treasure, and which form part of our culture and our life as necessary ideas and unavoidable expressions without which we cannot rule our behaviour nor direct our thinking; but which, limited and imperfect as they are, fall short of their object and narrow our views. However pure the gold of Yahweh's image might have been, the image could never reach the perfection of the model. Neither do our mental images. And the images of Yahweh divided Israel, as the concepts of God and of his work divide churches and religions today. Heavy upon our heads weighs still today the curse of Jeroboam, who taught Israel to sin.

There is no question of mistrusting the human intellect, and even less of avoiding dogma that defines the necessary truth; but there is definitely question of being aware of the essential limitation of human language, in order to use it with tact and to transcend it with generosity. Never to tie down ourselves to a golden calf. We must always move on in spirit and in prayer. After "Genesis" comes "Exodus", that is, after "generating" a new concept we must "exit" from it, which is what the very words mean in the history of

21

Israel and in the pilgrimage of our lives. We have to conceive the concept of God and live its reality in the way it is
given us; and then we have also to be ready to go beyond it,
however pleasant and familiar it may have become for us, in
order to enlarge experiences and open up visions on the
infinite truth we can never exhaust.

I come back to India for a while. The first Christian
missionaries were scandalized by the multitude of gods in
the Hindu pantheon (three hundred and thirty million is the
official figure), and they mercilessly castigated the colourful
"idolatry" that crowded the walls of the temples and the
pages of the scriptures of an age-old religion which was
spread through the length and breath of a whole subcontinent. There was a goddess who rode on a tiger, and a god
who slept on a snake, a monkey god and an elephant god, a
god who destroys what another god has created and a third
one preserves, their three faces united in stone in the
Elephanta caves off Bombay where they were used as bull's-
eyes by Portuguese gunners in shooting practice from their
men-of-war; while farther down in South Malabar other
"idols" were used by the children of Xavier's catechism as
targets too for other activities, if not so martial, no less
abusive and insulting. I do not judge the times, much less
the persons, and deliberately avoid the anachronism of
judging past events by present standards; I only record the
facts. What those great missionaries never suspected was that
the multiplicity of images was but another way, paradoxical-
ly opposite but similar in its effect, of saying exactly the same
thing that the prohibition of images had meant to say in
other lands and other scriptures: that there is no image that
could do justice to God, and that, consequently, either you
make none or you make thousands so that their very
multiplicity may proclaim their inability to describe him, and

22

God's transcendence be safeguarded by the variety of the colours. India's apparent polytheism is only the outside cover of a radical monotheism which no enlightened criticism can miss if it approaches it with the friendly desire to learn instead of the suspicion that comes from insecurity and leads to condemnation.

Hindu piety has a beautiful devotional practice: the slow rhythmical recitation of Vishnu's thousand names. The richness of Sanskrit lends itself to the coining of name after name with linguistic luxury and theological depth; the fabled and real Oriental memory learns them by heart in infallible order, and then the names are gently recited one by one, moving the lips slightly and with a faint sound even if one is alone in private recitation, to sacramentalize with the external gesture the love and the faith that surge in the soul at the contact with God. And the message is again the same: to say that God has a thousand names amounts to saying that he has none, or, in our expression, that he has a name "that is above all other names", and before it one may, either remain silent, or embark on the prolongued litany where thousand means eternity, and each name, as its turn comes, proclaims both its legitimacy, since it has been pronounced, and its failure, since it has to give way to the next. Each name brings with itself the message that it represents a genuine trait of him who has no traits, and that at the same time it has to withdraw and make room for another name in search of completion, since each is brief, limited, finite. Each name affirms and denies, speaks and falls silent, comes and goes. Hindu theologians have written long treatises on Vishnu's thousand names (as Fray Luis de Leon wrote his treatise on "The Names of Christ"), and many simple souls, without reading those treatises, repeat the sacred names with unfailing devotion. Every lover likes to repeat the name of the beloved.

23

The pity, even the tragedy, is that even this beautiful way of addressing God and singing his glories, can lose its message and forget its purpose, and often does so under human carelessness and lurking superstition. The thousand names, whose mission it was to remind us that there is no name by which we may exhaustively call God, become now themselves a name, longer and louder, but a name after all that now purports to be perfect, complete, final. People learn the thousand names by heart, recite them mechanically at the fall of the beads, repeat them without knowing what they say, and so eventually convert them into a formula, an incantation, a *mantra*, an image. Devotion ends in routine, and theology becomes a catalogue. Instead of a thousand names, a name made up of a thousand. The thousand names that had been excogitated to protect God's transcendence violate it even more grievously. The flow of titles, which was meant to remind us that no title is valid, has itself become a title, and Vishnu becomes a prisoner bound by the chain of a thousand links. That is image and parable of what happens in all religions and at all levels. The new idea, which for a start was an original conquest of a new feature of the God who has no features, itself becomes a routine, a fixed image, an idol. The photograph, fresh when it was first taken, becomes a page in an album; the butterfly, when caught for the collection, dies on a pin; the rose, when cut, withers and dies. Concepts also wither when filed away in the mind. To keep in contact with the living God, we have to renew the album.

SING A NEW SONG

A retreat director, with a long and rich experience behind him, used to say that the greatest obstacle for fervent religious in their yearly retreat is the memory of other retreats made in previous years, which have left a deep imprint in their religious career, and which inevitably come to mind when the annual retreat approaches, raise up the old ideal, make them long for its repetition and inspire in them the determination to do their outmost to revive the old fervour.

They will not. The person who approaches a retreat with such a disposition will neither make the present one nor the past one. The longing will continue: "That was a real retreat...!", the eyes will be turned back so as to make it impossible to see what is in front; the comparison, always unjust in itself, between that ideal director and this mediocre one will ruin all chances of spiritual profit, leading to frustration at losing the past which is no longer at hand, and missing the present which has been ignored.

In my young years as a religious I once made an exceptional retreat under the best director in the country, whose zeal and wisdom were certainly up to his reputation. The experience made a great impact on me..., and for years after that I dragged along with me the dead weight of having made a privileged retreat. I had taken detailed notes of every talk and, to make matters worse, someone else had done the same in even greater detail (I wonder now what kind of retreat that was where everybody seemed to have spent more time writing than praying!) and took the trouble to make copies and present them to a few of the elect so that they kept alive that fervour for ever. I stored carefully all the precious notes, and thought to myself: Splendid! I have now my annual retreat made for me for ever, and wherever I may be. Every year after that, when the time for the retreat arrived, I would unpack all the notes, consult them day by day, and revise them before each meditation...; I tried to work myself into a fervour with their memory... and only succeeded in getting bored with their repetition. I refused to learn new approaches since I already had with me the best approach. How to lower myself to lesser standards? Stupid pride which robbed me of much profit. It took me years to climb down from it. Until the day I took all those notes, tore them to pieces and threw them into the waste-paper basket, I was not free to make a fresh retreat, to live it again as a new reality instead of holding on to an old relic, venerable but dead. If we want to progress in the spirit it is essential to keep a wastebasket at hand.

I quote the orthodox archbishop Anthony Bloom: "To fix our mind in a past grace may make us miss a new grace. The God I knew yesterday is not necessarily the same that will reveal himself to me tomorrow. Do not live by memories. They are dead. God is alive. Ever new. Approach him with a sense of wonder. Conscious that you do not know him and he may bring a new face today. Do not

26

substitute your image of God formed by past experiences for God himself: this is spiritual idolatry. Repeat the prayer: 'Help me, Lord, to abandon all the false concepts I have of you.' What we must do is to collect all the knowledge of God which we possess in order to come into his presence, but then remember that all we know about God is our past, as it were, behind our back, and we are standing face to face with God in all his complexity, all his simplicity so close and yet unknown. Only if we stand completely open before the unknown, can the unknown reveal himself as he chooses to reveal himself to us as we are today. So, with this open-heartedness and open-mindedness, we must stand before God without trying to give him a shape or to imprison him in concepts and images, and then we must knock at the door."

We religious make a vow of poverty, and we apply it with greater or less generosity to material goods, to money and inheritances and bank accounts. That is a praiseworthy undertaking. But there is a much deeper and more radical poverty, the poverty of the soul and the detachment of the spirit, which applies to something much more precious to us and much harder to give up: our spiritual goods. Graces we have received, past experiences in prayer, glimpses of God and his Kingdom, understanding of eternal truths and ink-lings of realities to come. That is the treasure we value and appreciate most. And consequently we keep it in the safe-deposit vault of our memory and jealously protect its safety. That is spiritual greed and devotional hoarding. That is a clear trespassing on the naked poverty of soul and body which both the vow and the virtue require of the person who wants to approach God in perfect detachment. There are religious with a true and genuine vocation to the religious life and to spiritual heights within it who begin their journey, with enthusiasm but who later, frozen in the very same

27

graces which had helped them to start, cease to advance. To hold on to past graces amounts to being anchored in the past and missing the future. If we want to sail further into the sea and reach new shores, we have to weigh anchor and set sail, however hard it may be for us to leave the safe and comfortable harbour. Poverty of soul, the non-possession of former graces, is the best preparation to receive future ones.

I quote now C.S. Lewis, admired theologian, from whose works I would take whole paragraphs to learn by heart when I was studying English in India, fascinated by the beauty of his language and the originality of his ideas. "Many religious people lament that the first fervours of their conversion have died away. They may even try by pitiful efforts of will to revive what now seem to have been the golden days. But were those fervours—the operative word is *those*—ever intended to last? It would be rash to say that there is any prayer which God *never* grants. But the strongest candidate is the prayer we might express in the single word *encore*. And how should the Infinite repeat Himself? All space and time are too little for Him to utter Himself in them *once*. And the joke, or tragedy, of it all is that these golden moments in the past, which are so tormenting if we erect them into a norm, are entirely nourishing, wholesome, and enchanting if we are content to accept them for what they are, for memories. Properly bedded down in a past which we do not miserably try to conjure back, they will send up exquisite growths. Leave the bulbs alone, and the new flowers will come up. Grub them up and hope, by fondling and sniffing, to get last year's blooms, and you will get nothing. Unless a seed die…".

A great Christian gentleman told me once this story of his own life. Brought up since childhood in a great love of Jesus and devotion to Mary, he had occasion later in life to

28

go for the first time to Lourdes and visit, so to say, in her own house, Our Blessed Lady who had played a very important role always in his own life of faith. He went accordingly and visited the basilica, the gardens, the grotto; and while praying there before the image which he knew so well from so many holy pictures and which for the first time he was now seeing with his own eyes as it stood, white and blue, nested in the hollow of the witnessing rock, he realized that among the parallel benches arranged in front of the statue for the comfort and devotion of the faithful on their knees, half hidden by them on the ground, there was a small square slab, and on the slab this inscription in French: "Here was Bernardette standing when she saw Our Lady for the first time." He saw the slab and, with docile and devout gesture, he himself went close, stood on it silently and looked up at the statue. At that very moment, he said, he felt the heavens open on him with irresistible and sweet violence, his soul, his heart, his own senses were suddenly flooded with an unexpected and overwhelming joy essentially different from all joys he had ever felt on earth; and he experienced and lived for a while, which no human clock could time, the heavenly glory of which he had often heard and never before tasted. No need to say that the memorable visit remained engraved in his soul with permanent exclusiveness.

And now the second part of the story. Some years later he had again the opportunity to go to Lourdes, and again he awailed himself of it. He went to the village, the basilica, the grotto, sought the slab that had never faded from his memory, and with happy remembrance, with loving expectation, with a suspended feeling between curiosity and doubt, he went reverently towards it, stood on it in exact repetition of his former standing, looked up at the image of

Our Lady on the rock..., and... nothing happened. Or rather, yes, something important happened in the soul of that generous and enlightened Christian who already knew the ways of God and had learned a new lesson that day: God never repeats himself. God cannot be programmed, cannot be made to follow a procedure, cannot be tied down to time and place, does not accept set ways, does not like to tread twice the same path. God never "comes back", he simply "comes". Every time a new path, a new face..., a new slab. God never copies; he does not even copy himself. He can afford the luxury of being eternally different, and that is his very being. God is the one who never repeats himself (unless indeed he wants some time to repeat himself just to show that he does not even repeat the non-repetition). It is we men who endlessly repeat ourselves before our own impotence and everybody else's boredom. I am a writer and I know my sin: writing is repeating, because life (for man) is repetition. Not so for God, and that is why he is always to be sought outside all repetition. We have to change our slab.

The psalms know it and pray: "Sing to the Lord a new song." Only a new song can do justice and give glory to him whose very essence is to be for ever new.

Finally the quotation from Isaiah that always brings a thrill to my soul: "Remember not the things of the past; the things of long ago consider not. See, I am doing something new! Now it springs forth; do you not perceive it?" (43:18-19). Happy the eyes that see what you see.

30

THOU SHALT NOT TAKE
THE NAME OF THE LORD IN VAIN

If the second commandment on Moses' tablets was "You shall not make images of Yahweh", the third (second in our catechism) is "You shall not make wrong use of the name of Yahweh, your God." This commandment seeks the sanctification of man's word as the preceding one aimed at the sanctification of his thought. By not thinking or imagining anything unworthy of God, human thought gets trained and becomes ready not to think anything unworthy of any man or situation; and by not using his name unworthily, man's word is consecrated and pledges itself to speak the truth and pronounce justice. But we, who unwittingly break so often the first commandment, break also the second, and our lips "take in vain" the name of the Lord oftener than we ourselves realize.

The name, in Hebrew thought, stands for the person, and to misuse the name is to "use" the person, in this case "to use God"; and this explains why this offence comes immediately after the sin of idolatry that denied God. The name of Yahweh was used among his people with sacred efficacy in blessings and in curses, to give witness and to swear under oath. The frequency and importance of the use point to the facility of the abuse. He who purports to speak in the name of God can soon shift and begin to speak in his own name... while the subject in the sentence is still God, and grammar betrays theology. That is using God to one's own advantage, the ultimate insult of a mean mind.

Our language betrays us. "God knows that I have done this for your good alone." And you know that you have done it for your own interest alone. But one has to lean on words in order to impress the hearer and silence the opposition, and so God is mentioned first and his name presides over the sentence. "God knows that...". It is a safe trick, because God is not likely to speak and contradict us, while the solemn utterance of his name lends credibility to the verbal piety of the speaker. That is taking the name of the Lord in vain, that is using God and offending his majesty. That is breaking the third commandment of the law of Moses. "As God hears me...", "God is my witness that...", "I swear by God...". And truly God knows (this being now a legitimate use of the name of God!), God knows what is there behind that oath and that testimony and that solemn assertion. To cheapen God's name is dark prevarication.

Let's get closer home. "It is God's will for you that you should become a religious." Fine. But who are you to tell me so? Have you asked God? Has he told you so in private revelation for the good of my soul? You may well tell me that you think that I have a vocation for the religious life, and that I would be happy in that congregation which you appreciate as you appreciate me. You can even tell me that you would like very much to see me join, and that I would profit very much and would be able to do much good to others too if I joined. You can tell me all that, you can give

32

me your opinion and your advice and even voice your interest, and I will listen to you with respect and attention, and will keep in mind all that you say when I come to taking my own decision. But you have absolutely no right to say that such is God's will for me. You have no right to declare God's will for me, when what you call God's will may well be only your own opinion selfishly disguised under the name of God. Stop that unworthy mockery. Do not play God. Do not pose as a prophet. Do not take God's holy name in vain.

I believe in obedience, and I accept that the command of a legitimate superior can and does represent the will of God. Still I felt a shiver of disagreement when once, years and countries ago, I saw a certain religious provincial superior coming out of his office brandishing in his right hand a neatly typewritten sheet which contained all the new appointments of his subjects for that year, saying in a loud and triumphant voice, "Here is the will of God for our province this year!", and then adding in a sombre tone that was meant to underline the joke and make all laugh, "Now we shall see what is the will of men... Ha, ha, ha!" His subjects all laughed as expected. Ha, ha! (Was that also obedience?) The next instant they pounced upon the typewritten sheet, scanned nervously the names on it, breathed aloud when they did not find theirs..., and there and then began the yearly chorus of criticisms, ironies, prophecies, congratulations and remonstrations with which "the will of God" is traditionally greeted in the province.

Excuse me, dear Father Provincial. I acknowledge your authority and recognize that you take the place of God and act in his name. But for that very reason I ask you to respect that name and be worthy of the majesty you represent. Among the many qualities you doubtlessly possess, your capacity for dialogue is not precisely in evidence; you do not

33

take people easily into confidence, do not enjoy consulta-
tions, do not give time and interest to the rounds of meetings
and conversations with the people concerned. You tend to
be authoritarian in your decisions, while obedience, at least
as we understand it today, is rather a process, a discernment, a common task and mutual confidence in which both
the superior and the subject remain always open to each
other and to God in the complex search of what is best for
the person and for the common work. And it could well be
that, unawares to yourself, you hide the evidence of your in-
competence behind the shield of your authority. For me that
typewritten sheet is not, by itself, God's will, even if has
come from your typewriter and you may have typed it
yourself. Sincerely, Father Provincial, it does not ring true.
You yourself know fully well that the list will have to be
changed and modified several times until its final edition.
Please, do not boast on the first day, do not proclaim, do
not threaten, do not wave your sheet in the air with easy
triumphalism. Do not speak of God's will yet. Wait and
listen, have patience and "obedience" which you too must
have to the circumstances and the persons, and through
them to God who manifests himself in them, and only then
make humbly known what you believe to be the will of God,
with all the limitations of your understanding... and of your
typewriter.

To misuse God's holy name. The sin of the clergy, the
sin of priests and religious, precisely because we feel closer
to God, and our daily familiarity with him makes us believe
we have the right to use his name in place of ours. And
therefore this commandment is God's commandment for his
Church and its officials, for his representatives, for those
who speak in his name, for those who declare his will with
authority. Daily commandment reflected in the daily prayer

"holy be your name", as urgent as the "daily bread" that follows, so as to uphold the majesty of God's name, immortal sustenance of our souls, as the sustenance of our bodies too is upheld, and God's will be done (in word and in deed) on earth as it is in heaven.

In the city where I live there is a tailor, true to his trade both in the elegance of his cut and in the unreliability of his deliveries. After completing the trials for a suit, when asking him when it will be ready, he thinks for a moment, as though calculating (or perhaps praying) in his mind, and then he solemnly announces: "If it is God's will... next Monday." Pious soul that he is! There is always an oil lamp burning before the colourful image of his family God, he fans it with the perfume of incense sticks when opening the shop every morning, and touches briefly to its feet the measuring tape before taking the measurements of the client. So when the moment comes to fix the date for the delivery he cannot but think of God and submit his calculations to his will: "If God wants... by Monday." The client is duly impressed by the sudden mention of God, and accepts the appointment with liturgical reverence. On Monday he comes and asks for his suit. The tailor, without change in his pious countenance, answers softly: "It is not yet ready...; it was not God's will." To whom does the client complain? To the tailor or to God? It is obvious that if it had been God's will that the suit be ready for Monday, it would have been so; and if it is not ready it is because it has been God's will that it should not be, and before that there is no possible complaint. The tailor is right. When can it then be ready? "If God wants it so... by Thursday." And so the game goes on. The tailor manages to keep both his devotion and his customers, and his skill with the needle makes his clients put up with his irresponsible handling of the calendar. Before that tailor one would have

35

to stand up and make him face the facts: Please, do not mix your profession with your devotion. Leave God out of this for a while, and do not bother about when he wants the suit to be ready, rather say plainly when are you ready to deliver it. You know how many days you need and how much work you have, you know when you can finish the work and when you are ready to do so. Then say it and do it. Monday or Thursday, fix the date and stick to it. Do not justify your delays by bringing in the divine providence. Do not take the name of the Lord in vain.

Another example, more serious, even tragic this time; ... and let him who has never stumbled in this throw the first stone. In a village I know well, not far from my own city, worked many years as parish priest in its small Catholic minority a companion of mine, a man of great zeal both religious and social, full of resources in his rich personality and his organizational powers to serve his needy parishioners not only in the care of their souls, but also in the essential relief of their extreme poverty. As he succeeded in obtaining for them a certain measure of financial independence, and freedom from the deadly grip of exploiters and money-lenders, he inevitably clashed with the oppressors, and particularly so with a local boss whose own selfish interests were threatened by the social work of the parish priest. The boss decided to attack the parish priest and harass him to try to make him cow down and leave the place. He bought false witnesses, cooked up wrong charges, and dragged that good and kindly man from court to court without respite. He could prove nothing against him, but he persisted all the more in his campaign of threats and charges to get rid of him. Everybody in the village knew that it was all a mean plot of wicked lies, and they deplored the moral torture their beloved benefactor was going through; but they were unable

36

to do anything to help him. In the midst of that situation a piece of news reached the village. The only son of that arrogant boss had died in a car accident. And the immediate comment that came out unanimously from the lips of all in the village, Christians, Hindus and Muslims, was: God has punished him!

I respect the feelings of those good people, and the popular mentality that spoke in them and saw justice done in the family trial that had befallen a man they considered wicked. But I reject the hasty verdict, the irresponsible condemnation, the sentence of divine justice on the lips of man: God has punished him. Who are you to know that, and who are you to say that? To begin with, it seems to me a strange kind of justice that kills the innocent son in order to punish his guilty father. If justice was to be done, could not the car accident have been so arranged that the father, and not the son, should die in it? That is a first consideration. But the main point that I want to set down, clear and firm, is that even if the father had died in the accident, even then nobody would have had the right to say, God has punished him. No man knows the depths of man's conscience, and no man knows the judgement of God. No one knows which of God's actions is punishment and which is purification, which is trial and which is compassion. Neither I nor anybody nor even the whole people together have any authority to decide and declare that an accident is punishment, and a death is penalty. It is for me to keep silent before suffering and to respect death, not to pose as God and proclaim with culpable ease his secret judgements. "God has punished him." With that declaration God becomes an instrument of my own opinions, and even, on occasion, of my hatred and my vengeance. If suffering befalls anyone I dislike, and I say "God has punished him", I

37

set the seal of divine justice on what is purely my own feeling of jealousy and personal vengeance. Deep in my soul I rejoice at a rival's discomfiture, but since I do not want to admit before others nor before myself that I take pleasure in my neighbour's harm, I set up God's name first and say "God has punished him", when what I actually feel and do not confess is, "I am happy that my enemy suffers". That is manipulating God, misusing his name and usurping his throne. And even then I will not tell him who does that... "God will punish you!" "Leave to God what to God belongs" said solemnly and decisively his Son.

THOU SHALT NOT MANIPULATE
THE LORD YOUR GOD

The commandment is the same, but I give it now a new twist, hinted at in the preceding chapter, which will lead us to a deeper understanding of the role that different concepts of God play in our lives. Making a wrong use of the name of God is trying to manipulate him. The concept of a God who is close to us, friendly and intimate, may generate such confidence and familiarity that the door may be opened for the temptation to manipulate him. Friendship with God may degenerate into camaraderie, and closeness into insolence. Manipulating a man is the ultimate outrage against the dignity of the human person, and trying to manipulate God is blasphemy in action. Yet such an attitude, unfortunately, is not quite so rare, and it is important to unmask it in order to avoid it.

People wanted to manipulate Jesus again and again during his public years. They asked him for "signs", for wonders and miracles just as a curiosity, as entertainment, as a condition to save his life. "Do here among us what you have done in other cities", "They asked him for a sign from

39

heaven", "Herod expected to witness a miracle, and in-
sisted in many ways", the crowd cried "Come down from
the cross, and we'll believe in you!" They believed that Jesus
would perform miracles whenever they asked him, in order
to establish his prestige, to prove his mission, to save his life.
Jesus' reaction was to call such people a "wicked and
adulterous generation", and to keep his peace in quiet dignity
before Herod. Jesus will not allow himself to be manipulated
by anybody... even if that costs him his life.

On a special occasion Jesus was threatened by a more
subtle manipulation. One of his disciples enjoyed a special
friendship with him, and, he himself or his mother—the
evangelists disagree—tried to take advantage of the situation
to obtain a concrete favour. "Grant that these two sons of
mine may sit, one at your right hand and one at your left, in
your kingdom." That is an occasion when Jesus' reaction
disappoints me. He excuses himself saying that such a decision belongs to the Father, not to him, as though he were
saying, "I would most willingly grant that to you, but, I'm
sorry, it is not in my power to do so"; whereas I, in the
smallness of my understanding and in the cultural environment I live in, would much have preferred (and I make bold
to speak my mind because I reverently respect Jesus' right to
speak his) that he would have faced her directly and told
her, in his own delicate way and language, that he would
not allow anybody to manipulate him, not even the beloved
mother of his favourite friend. Maybe he did think so, only
he did not speak out to spare the feelings of his disciple's
mother. In any case he certainly rejected the appeal in the
strongest way he knew, which was the recourse to his
Father's authority. God will not be manipulated. When the
attempt to corner the first places in the coming kingdom
leaked to the group, there was trouble among the apostles.

40

Man notices at once when a rival pretends to manipulate someone on whom he too depends, senses the danger and registers his protest. Jesus had to speak for a long time to his disciples that evening.

Jesus' bold promise, "ask and you shall receive", places in our hands an awesome instrument of faith and an abundance of favours and graces which, by its very generosity, lays us open to the temptation of trying to manipulate God, to use God's promise to press him into giving us something which he simply does not want to give. The danger is not that God may in fact be manipulated, which will never and can never happen, but that we may attempt it, and in doing so may lower again the concept of God to merely human levels. And lowering the concept of God, I repeat, is lowering life.

Here is a personal experience which came close to causing a crisis in my life. Among my students at the university there was a Hindu boy to whom my attention had been drawn from the beginning by the physical and moral suffering I knew he was enduring. He suffered from double vision in his eyes, which neither spectacles nor operation could correct, and which caused him sharp daily headaches that started in the morning, increased during the day, and became unbearable at night in a fateful cycle of misery and helplessness. To make matters worse his family, which took his sufferings as God's punishment ("God has punished you!"), blamed him for his misery, made life impossible for him, to the extent that once he had run away from home so that his family might be humiliated when all the neighbours came to know of his flight, and he might be avenged. I took a great interest in that young man who suffered so much, and did for him all that the zeal and fervour of my youthful priesthood inspired me to do. I prayed for him, prayed with

41

him, laid my hands on him, offered sacrifices and penances for him. I wanted to make way for the Gospel in my surroundings, and I reminded the Lord that whenever he sent his disciples to proclaim the Good News he gave them also the companion power to heal the sick, and that he himself had come to say on a formal occasion: "What is easier, to tell this paralytic, 'Your sins are forgiven', or to tell him, 'Get up and walk!'?" And if I, as a priest, had the higher power to forgive sins, how was it I did not have the easier one to heal the sick? If "signs" were to follow those who believed and thus his message was to spread according to his promise, how were people to believe without signs, particularly in a case so worthy of care and mercy as that young man? My arguments with the Lord, prayers and offerings went for nothing. Time passed, and my young friend only got worse.

One day, however, he appeared in my room exuding joy and happiness, his smiling eyes proclaiming that their vision was now normal, his radiant face announcing before he could open his mouth that all his troubles were over, that he was now a happy man in body and soul, full of life and bursting with youth. What had happened? I understood in a flash before he could speak. I noticed his clothes were saffron in colour, and I saw round his neck a string of black beads, from which hung a medallion that framed an image I knew well. That was the photo of a Hindu guru who set his followers three conditions to ensure their happiness in this world and their salvation in the next: they had to dress in saffron (India's sacred colour), had to wear his photo round their necks, and had to change their name for a new one he would give them. My young friend, Vinay, informed me that from then on he would be called Swami Amrutsiddhant, and everything was explained. He had gone to that guru, had pledged loyalty to him, and all his troubles, moral and physical, had disappeared on the spot. Before my astonished eyes stood a healthy young man, full of life and zest as I had always dreamt he would be one day... only by another way. "There is only one thing missing", he told me with a mischievous smile while he showed me his undershirt which was still white, "I have not yet found a saffron undershirt; as soon as I get one, I'll put it on, and my joy will be complete." Amen.

My feelings were all in a mess as I looked at him. Relief and joy to see the sudden happiness of someone I loved, astonishment to see splendid health where for months and months I had only seen misery in body and soul, surprise before the saffron and the medallion, and deep down uneasiness and even hidden anger and protest to see that a Hindu guru had succeeded where a Catholic priest had failed. I have a deep and sincere respect for Hindu gurus in general, and real veneration for some who are truly holy men and genuine mystics in the highest regions that are given to the human spirit to attain. But the guru of the medallion was somewhat different. He had just then published a book whose title "From Sex to Superconsciousness" defended his thesis that mystical ecstasies could only be reached through sexual intercourse; and that was precisely the reason I had refused to preside over a series of conferences he was giving during his stay in our city, a slight for which he never quite forgave me. He indulged in some practices which I could not reconcile with a commitment to the spiritual life and which his own disciples found difficult to accept or explain. He was highly controversial to say the least. And it was this guru who had cured my friendly young man.

I accept, I told the Lord, that you are eternally free, that you are not bound by the code of canon law, that you can distribute your graces outside the seven sacraments, beyond the Church you yourself founded and through any means or person you may freely choose. You are Father of all, and all come under your power and your love. That is clear and definite. However, together with that, you will have to agree that I have made a fool of myself in this affair. The boy is sensible and, anyhow, he is already cured, and he tells me that out of gratefulness he is now going to America to prepare his guru's advent in more productive countries; and do keep protecting him as you have done now. What concerns me here is to find out what is it you are trying to tell me with this action of yours. For him your message has been the glory of his healing; for me it has been rather the concrete revelation of your supreme freedom when dealing with men, your solemn refusal to adapt yourself to our expectations of you, your enjoyment in breaking moulds and standards, and your absolute resistance to being manipulated by anybody in any way. That is what I, to some extent, was doing, wasn't I? It all was for your greater glory and honour, of course, but in fact I had already traced out for you in advance the plan of all that you had to do with that boy. You had only to follow my instructions, and all would be fine. I had caught you with quotations from your own Gospel, I had hinted that if you wanted to find a way into the world I live in, here you had a good occasion which I would then properly make use of for your own glory. I had everything ready for you. Only your signature was needed. And instead of duly signing on the dotted line, you send me to go cool my heels. Apparently you do not enjoy it when other people make plans for you, when they fix the details for you, they tell you what you have to do, they manipulate you. Understood. For me that lesson is more important than the cure of the boy. I do not know how he and his bizarre guru will fare in remote countries, but I do know that from

44

now on I, for my part, intend to respect more your judgements and your independence. Here you have me right in the field, full of energy, and ready at your service. Deal with me as you please. You are the head and you know what you want to do and how. Forgive my insolence when I pretended to make you follow my own plans. I believe that I understand you a little better now, and you know that I appreciate immensely any chance of knowing you better, because I know that your knowledge is the source of all good.

I accuse myself of having tried to manipulate God again and again in my plans and in my dreams, in my zeal and in my impatience, in my efforts to impose on him my way of thinking and my hurry for acting. I accuse myself of having made up for my own use an easy God, a docile, obliging, obedient God, reflection of my own ambitions, condition of my success and instrument of my glory. I accuse myself of having manufactured a pocket god, cheap and convenient and comfortable. I accuse myself of having spoken in the name of God, thought in the name of God, acted in the name of God when in reality I was thinking and speaking and acting purely in my own name. I accuse myself of having faked his signature and stolen his seal. And I accept and welcome the lesson he taught me through an outlandish guru. That was only the beginning of many lessons. There was still much more to learn.

45

WHY DON'T WE ALL BECOME ATHEISTS?

In the Lincoln monument in Washington, on the wall to the right as one climbs the steps, there are carved in bold letters some words of the historic president in which he refers to the American civil war and says: "Both sides read the same Bible, and both prayed to the same God and expected from him victory for their own armies and defeat for their adversaries." There, in the stone of the monument and in the sincerity of a president who spoke with a sense of history, has remained the expression of the saddest manipulation to which man ever in his blind egoism has submitted God. To kill each other in his name. And that was not only in a war of the past. It still happens today again and again in the old continent and in the new, in the Orient, both near and far; indeed anywhere where God's name is invoked... and abused. In a certain country the two fighting bands have claimed opposite apparitions of Our Lady..., each one condemning, of course, the opposite band. One has to justify one's own cause at all cost, and the final approval is sought in the blessing of the God of hosts. Each war becomes a crusade, the victims are martyrs, and eternal glory is promised to those who die on the battle front. The

47

holy war. Such were the wars of the Israelites, and such were the wars of Islam. And the wars against Islam. Even in civil wars people fight "for God and country". Which country? If one may ask. And the echo of that question rings with even deeper and more pathetic irony: and, which God? Wars made in the name of God end up by generating atheism.

I am on the terrace of the students' hostel in our own college campus on the outskirts of the city of Ahmedabad. On either side of me, as I lean on the railing towards the side that looks towards the city, are several students, all of us intently gazing at the familiar skyline which today has something new and tragic about it. Our eyes are held by the horizon before us. Suddenly a boy shouts, "Another one! Look there!" We all look in the direction of his extended arm, and see what he sees. Another cloud of smoke. Black and dense in round ashen strokes over the cement line. Where could that be? We conjecture the area, the street, the building by familiar landmarks. And before we finish our conjectures..., another one! and another! Nobody counts any more the columns of smoke, as they already blend with each other to create a deadly curtain over the hapless landscape. The city is burning. Oh dear city, beloved and cherished through years of intimacy in the labyrinth of your streets and in the history of your walls, city of Gandhi, city of peace, city with a Muslim name and a Hindu tradition where both religions have coexisted through centuries street by street and shoulder to shoulder! Why do your houses burn today, why does your asphalt blush with blood and your sky grow dark with mourning?

Wars of religion. Islam entered India at the stroke of the sword. Soon the races settled down and history got under way. Old wounds healed, and coexistence grew. It had been

48

working now for centuries. But from time to time winds from the past blow on the embers, and the flames leap up again. Someone stones a cow, sacred to the Hindus, or someone drives a pig, impure for the Muslims, through one of their processions. And the old blood surges again... and runs through the streets. And then the vengeance. And vengeance upon vengeance. The never ending cycle. And all in God's name. Allah-O-Akbar! Jai Mahakali! Battle cries of an unholy heritage. Endemic tragedy that strikes city after city in relentless agony. Recurring violence in a land of peace.

We are still on the terrace looking at the sad shadows in the sky. Some of the students are Hindus, some Muslims, other Christians. We find it painful to look, but we cannot tear ourselves from the sight. We are far from the centre of the city and can still contemplate in temporary safety the smoke belt that encompasses the horizon. Another cloud of smoke! When will the fire subside? When will hatred stop? When will man be man again?

We hardly speak among ourselves, and that is why I hear better and am struck deeper by the question one of the boys by my side asks me: "Father, if we kill one another because we belong to different religions, would it not be better if we all became atheists?" All of us have heard what he has said, and nobody answers him. On that same terrace we meet every Saturday night for an hour, all hostelites together under the stars, and we pray and meditate, I speak to them about God and love and virtue and goodness, and we all sing religious songs, keep long silences and feel together and offer up to God our brotherhood. But what is the use of all that pious brotherhood of Saturday night, when from that same terrace the next day we see the smoke of human hatred rising in the name of the same God we

49

have been invoking there? All my sermons and all our prayers during the year have vanished before that single question, sad and unavoidable: If we kill one another in God's name, would it not be better if we all became atheists?

There is another Father by my side who whispers in my ear: "There you have it; that is what pagans are at heart; always fighting among themselves." I answer without looking at him: "What's currently happening in Ireland between Catholics and Protestants?" We all keep quiet again. When religion joins politics, blood flows—in the East and in the West. The name of God, which should make us all brothers, makes us kill each other. Religious wars. Prayers for victory, that is for killing. A day will come, said Jesus, when men will kill you thinking they are doing God a service. They still think that way. They still keep killing. Today the beating hearts of conquered warriors are not offered before the holy stone of Uitzilopochtli's Aztecan cult; now we do it with hand grenades and submachine guns; but the rubrics are the same. We still kill in the name of God.

Mahatma Gandhi, the greatest soul of our age ("a time will come", said Einstein, "when people will refuse to believe that such a one as this ever walked the earth") united the whole of India in the peaceful revolution that gave freedom without war to the greatest colony in the world from the greatest power in the world. But he had to pay a posthumous price for his noble enterprise. Truly ecumenical at heart, and an equal brother to Hindus and to Muslims, he nevertheless used, as motto and ideal for the free state he fought for, a somewhat loaded word: Ram-rajya. In itself it is a beautiful word which means "kingdom of God", a traditional expression in India which appealed to the religious feelings of the people, united all the castes, and converted the independence movement into a sacred crusade. The only

50

trouble was that the word "God" in the expression is idiomatically the word "Rama", which makes reference to a concrete incarnation of the Hindu faith, not easily acceptable to an orthodox Muslim. There, in symbol and slogan, though very much against the definite wishes of the Mahatma, was the seed of discord. From that religious split— together with an infinite web of human and political motives of which history knows—emerged Pakistan in a surgical operation that bled the subcontinent; and from there too continue to come out those columns of smoke that blacken with painful regularity the blue sky of the cities of India. A sacred word was joined to an earthly enterprise, God's name was pronounced in a political uprising, however just in its demands and restrained in its moderation..., and today from the terrace of our hostel we witness the unavoidable result of the enmity between those who call God Rama and those who call him Allah. And I have to listen with theological sadness to the heartfelt comment of that young college student: "Wouldn't it be better if we all became atheists?"

That was the first time I "heard" atheism. The first time I was listening to the atheistic option in the live word of a concrete person before a serious situation which made the proposition not sound absurd. It was not a chapter in a textbook, not a thesis to refute in an examination, not a syllabus for "dialogue" or the ideological manifesto of a political party; it was an almost logical conclusion from real premises we all had before our eyes. The short-term premises were the smoke, the fire and the blood; but the long-term premise, the hidden but fundamental premise, the original fallacy and the radical abuse from which all the evil derived was the manipulation of God's name. A well-meant but limited concept of God had given rise, through history and prejudices

51

and misunderstandings, to the possibility of its being used for causes which, though just in themselves, become dangerous when God is made to fight under the party's banner. The temptation to use God (or the negation of God, which amounts to the same) has always been close to political ambition, and is still so in our days. In all continents and in quite diverse ideologies, God is used to justify party objectives. For a while it may even help the cause. In the long run it harms the faith. Manipulation of God is the seed of atheism.

THE GOD OF THE FOOTBALL POOLS

From the "manipulated God" I now pass on to the "God in the gap". That is another concept of God which is almost unavoidable in our dealings with him, is even temporarily useful as it has some partial truth in it, but is dangerous and harmful in the long range as it is essentially incomplete, twisted and false. To see how very common the idea is and how wrong it nevertheless is, it is enough to mention it. It comes to this: so long as I am in control of the situation, and my resources (are they really "mine"?) are enough to meet it, I handle it on my own and do not "trouble" God nor think of him; however, as soon as the situation gets out of my hands, as soon as I run into a crisis, a serious problem, something that goes beyond my possibilities and does not yield to my resources, then I run to God, implore his help and light candles before his image. So long as life goes on by itself (or does it really?), there is nothing to worry about; but as soon as the "gap" appears and I cannot fill it up, I have recourse to God that he may repair it or may take me in his arms and pass me safely to the other side. That is the function of the "God in the gap", a title that is not found in manuals of devotion or liturgical

53

books, but which many faithful in all religions devoutly and regularly invoke.

There is a popular saying in Spanish: "If you want to learn how to pray, sail far into the sea." On land, where one can step strong and walk without fear, there is no need to pray; I manage by myself, and there is no reason for me to think of God at every step. But on the high seas, when the winds blow, the waves rise and the tempest rages; when the boat pitches and rolls and is flooded with water, and I see the sailors struggle and cannot even hear their voices in the thunder... I can only think of God, turn to him and implore his help. Fishermen all over the world have always been particularly religious people. They live near the gap.

In the Indian languages we have a different proverb with a similar meaning: "When business goes well, we think of the jeweller; when it goes badly, we think of God." That is the most dangerous definition of God: God is he whom we think of when things go badly. There is, of course, some positive value in that attitude, namely the recognition (however reluctant) of the fact that God can help us when nobody else can; and that act of faith (however unwilling) has after all its own value which it is only fair to admit; the true friend shows himself in the moment of crisis, and our very turning spontaneously to God when trouble comes, implicitly proves that we consider him to be our best friend, as he is indeed. But there is also something seriously wrong in the attitude that relegates God to the bad moments of life, makes of prayer a bitter medicine for sickness instead of a joyful drink for life, confines faith to emergencies, and reduces religion to a first-aid post. Life is not made up of gaps, and limiting God's action to the gaps is unworthy and unfair. That is surely not the way he wants to be dealt with.

54

I have been a teacher for many years, and as such have been in contact with generations of students who have passed through my class, most of whom disappear into oblivion year after year, with only an occasional reminder at an old-students gathering, or an invitation to a wedding or the opening of a new clinic or bureau, with a name on it which I vaguely remember and read again with pleasure, happy that an old acquaintance should remember me in a significant moment in his life, all the more so if he or she comes in person to renew the old contact. What I do not enjoy so much is the sudden appearance of an old student, who has kept absolutely no contact with me for five or ten years, and who now turns up casually as it first seems, starts talking in smiles and praises of his days as a student and of the good time (?) he had in my class, makes me believe for a while that he has come only to remember the good old days and thank me for them..., and when he rises to take leave he just remembers, almost by chance, that, yes, he had something in mind, and, by the way, wanted to ask me a little favour, a recommendation letter for a place where he knows my name counts, a speech at the inaugural function of his new premises, an article for the silver-jubilee souvenir of the association over which he so worthily presides. And then I feel like telling him: All these long years you never once thought of coming to see me; and now that you need me, you rush here. Great! I can see your good old days and your deep gratitude! You are just playing with me, and trying to hoodwink me. Yes, certainly, I will come for the inauguration and write the article and send the testimonial..., and will take leave of you till the next time you happen to need me. I will do what you want, but let it be clear that I do not believe in your affection or in your gratitude. You have used me, you have placed me as a bridge over a "gap" in your life, and I have not enjoyed the experience. A person-to-person relationship cannot be built on mutual indigence.

55

Another danger of "the religion of the gap" is that, as man understands the universe better and material progress advances, the number of gaps inevitably decreases. For primitive man everything in life was a gap: the lightning that struck him, the floods that ravaged his fields, the plague that decimated his tribes; which is why the Greeks needed a god of thunder, the Egyptians worshipped the Nile, the Hindus attributed smallpox to a goddess. Today there is inoculation against smallpox, damns on the Nile, and lightning-rods on the top of every tall building; which means in turn that so many gods have lost their jobs. Gaps are being filled up; that is, God's intervention in the life of man is being limited more and more. True, there is still always the gap of death, which is not easily filled up; the fear of an afterlife, the tremor before judgement, and the weight of eternity; and that gives us some reassurance that the thought of God will never quite disappear from the minds of mortal men. But it would be sad to reduce God's presence to death notices and funeral parlours. The theology of the gap can never give us a living God to fill our hearts and gladden our lives. The concept is defective, and a defective concept of God is a source of harm.

I even once discovered the God of the football pool, or the God of the lottery. It happened this way. I had gone to the house of a very religious family where I sat down, chatted, took tea, and noticed that in a corner of the living room there was a sacred statue, and on the folded hands of the statue there was a piece of paper someone had obviously placed there. I felt curious, though I did not show it, I took advantage of the moment of leave-taking to close in on to the image and take a quick glance at the paper. Right enough. The carefully folded paper in the hands of the holy image was a lottery ticket. I understood it all. The pious

56

family. The high cost of living. The secular providence of the state lottery. The neutral indifference of the lucky number. Something that was not in the hands of man (lottery draws being reputedly free from cheating), and that consequently was purely and exclusively in the hands of God. Let us pray to him then, and let us make it easy for him to hear our prayers and satisfy our needs. Just a little push in time, one more turn of the drum, the right ball with the right number comes out... and we all live happily ever after. That was the meaning of the folded paper in the hands of the statue. My curiosity had been satisfied, and I promptly left.

I want to express my full respect (and even holy envy) for that simple devotion, and for the right which Jesus gave and every person has to ask of God whatever he wants. But respect for devotional practices is compatible with a sense of humour, chiefly when humour becomes a lighthearted way of doing theology. What I have in mind is the rather embarrassing problem that lottery ticket is causing almighty God. What is he going to do with it? Give it the prize? But, isn't that cheating? Besides, this is not the only ticket for which prayers have been offered. There are other families, just as pious and as needy, that have thought the same thought and prayed the same prayer. What to do then? Cast lots among all those who have prayed? That would be another lottery. But the most serious aspect of the problem is that if God decides to give the first prize to the ticket that hangs from his hands in the statuette, word would soon get around,... and there would not be enough religious statues in the whole country to meet the deadline of the next draw! On the other hand, if God ignores the prayers and leaves the ticket without even a refund, what happens to his promise "ask and you shall receive" so often and so insistently repeated throughout the Gospels? Whatever he does, he is in trouble, that is, those who have such a concept of him will be in trouble, or perhaps not they themselves in their happy simplicity, but those who see the situation and think and reflect and draw conclusions and want to keep the concept of God as pure as possible in the minds of men, in order to safeguard his majesty and extend his kingdom. It is more important to have the right concept of God than to hit the jackpot in a lottery. Some people may even draw comfort from the thought that so long as there are lotteries and football pools, there will be people who think of God. I hereby resolve to find out whether there are lotteries and football pools in atheistic countries, and what people there do with the tickets. There surely must be something they hang them from.

This little episode, which is strictly historical, had an unexpected epilogue, also strictly historical, which may help in the mutual understanding between religions I foster and stand for. I returned home that day after the visit, and in the informal exchange of daily happenings I spoke about my experience and my own reflections on it with my companions in the priesthood and the religious life. One of them was quick to put in his own comment (this happened in India): "Typical elementary superstition of pagans and their gods!" I answered: "Sorry, Father. It was precisely a Catholic family, and the image was that of Our Lady of Mount Carmel." In some things all religions come fairly close together.

By the way, their ticket did not fetch any prize.

IF JESUS HAD BEEN BORN IN INDIA

"If Jesus had been born in India, what concept of God would he had preached?" The question was asked me by my friend Kakasaheb Kalelkar, thinker and writer, Mahatma Gandhi's right hand in the field of education, ideal partner for any religious talk, who, whenever his constant journeys (he used to say he lived in the train) brought him to Ahmedabad, would call me to breakfast with him, since nobody visited at that early hour, and we could talk at leisure of the themes we both loved. "I admit the New Testament", he continued, "because I admit Jesus; but there is no reason why I should be made to accept the Old Testament as well. That is, I keep the Hindu scriptures, the Vedas and Upanishads, in place of the Old Testament, and on them I ground and understand the New Testament and Jesus in it. Do you follow me?"

The idea was as simple as it was bold. Not quite new, however. Gandhiji himself, apostle of the Sermon on the Mount, could not, for all his goodwill, handle the Old Testament, and in his reading of it did not go beyond the Book of Numbers (such a pity! It is one of the most revealing books

59

in the whole Bible if properly understood...); and his disciple Kalelkar was now drawing the conclusion and proposing a change of roots in the Biblical tree. A direct graft of the Gospel on the trunk of the Vedas. "Why should I become a Hebrew?" he was asking me. "Why should we be circumcised?" asked the first Greek converts. The way to make Jesus truly universal is to let him be incarnated in each religious scripture and in each theological tradition so that his own figure would be enhanced, and the whole world would be the better for it. Thus we launched hypotheses while we partook of his favourite breakfast of germinated green pulse, their growing tails showing shyly out of the tender cotyledon. He was radically vegetarian, and one day refused to accept even a biscuit in our house for fear it might contain eggs. Not a chance! I assured him in vain.

Hinduism proposes three "models" of God to the consideration of its followers. I use here the word "model" almost in its mathematical sense. The set of ideas, equations, graphs, postulates, deductions that describe in mathematical terms a given situation of the physical world, of the stock exchange, of the human behaviour or even of the human body's reaction to a particular virus, and thus help to foresee somehow the development of the system in question and to work more easily within it. No model is exact; they are only abstract approximations to concrete realities, but their study facilitates the understanding of life's phenomena, simplifies their expression and promotes their applications. All this applies to the conceptual "models" of God I am reviewing here as they come up. They are ways of defining God without which we cannot refer to him or enter into relationship with him, but which, if we mistake them for the infinite reality they represent, can defeat their own purpose and harm the very relationship we want to improve.

60

I say that there are three fundamental models in Hinduism. The God of devotion, the God of negation, and the God of action. There is a very elaborate terminology in the matter, but I skip it. I go to the point. The God of devotion whom Hinduism presents is the most similar to the God of the Christian tradition. He has all the features that are familiar to us: creation, omnipotence, love, providence, intimacy, incarnation. In Hindusm are also found prophecies of the coming of the redeemer, miraculous birth, killing of the innocents, miraculous deeds in favour of the poor and the oppressed, moral preaching and violent death. Remarkable parallel with Christianity, though serious conceptual differences remain within it. Maybe not all my readers know that in India too devout people build "cribs", not only to Jesus at Christmas, but to Krishna on *Janmashtami* (which means "nativity", because *janma* is "birth"). Also Krishna is born at midnight, is worshipped by shepherds, carols are sung to him, and the faithful strive to imitate the love his mother Yashoda and his father (who has not fathered him) Nanda have for him. He is God as a child, a friend, a lover, a companion; a God who helps, encourages and stays through life by man's side. The "way of devotion" is, according to the Hindu spiritual masters, the easiest, most common and most universal of all the ways that lead to God, and it is practised as such in a thousand ways and manners, with feasts and pilgrimages and joy and colour through the length and breadth of India. If Jesus had been born in India we could have had a Christian religion fairly similar in actual practice to the one we have—carols and all.

But there are other ways. The "way of knowledge" corresponds to the model of the "God of negation". Here God leaves our side, goes far away, becomes impersonal,

61

escapes all images and all concepts, and to "know" him consists in knowing that we "do not know" him. The repeated formula *neti-neti* ("not this, not this") leads to a total detachment, of the senses first and of the understanding later, from the urge to apprehend God in their moulds. It is not this, go ahead; it is not this, search farther on. Mystical ladder, cloud of unknowing, departure in the night with John of the Cross. Hardly have I had an experience, a contact, a religious enlightenment which I want to grasp, to treasure, to inscribe in my memory and repeat in my conduct, when a secret voice tells me in my ear: Not this, not this; let it pass, let it go; don't hold on to it, don't grab it; give thanks for it, but don't stop at it; appreciate what you have received, but don't get stuck in it and move on. To deny in order to affirm. To ignore in order to know. To understand nothing in order to understand everything. Total detachment, asceticism in concepts, austerity of thought. "He who wants to save his life, will lose it; but whoever loses it for my sake, will find it." Premise for a paradox, with its ultimate consequence drawn.

The paradox is that from saying No to everything we pass smoothly to saying Yes to everything. The ends meet, the snake bites its own tail (favourite Hindu symbol), the eternal wheel goes round and round. There was nothing of which we could say that it was God, and so, with irrefutable Oriental logic, we end up by saying that everything is God. Pantheism, monism, *advaita*. The theology of the "One-without-a-second". All is one. All is God. And I with it. I am Brahma. That is the final creed and the last confession of the "way of knowledge". To know myself, in my own finitude and limitation and smallness which I know only too well, united now and identified with the divine essence that fills the cosmos, as a pulsation of the universe, a gentle breeze of stellar wind.

62

In my fervour to understand and explain other people's attitudes and beliefs ever since I came to India, I even came to accept risks and brave dangers a little beyond what one could afford in those hardy preconciliar days. One day I went almost too far. I was defending at a public function before professors and students some theological theses of comparative religion, and I delved confidently into the intricacies of the "I am Brahma", trying to project from inside the central posture of orthodox Hinduism with genuine enthusiasm. That was a little too much for the president of the session, faithful guardian of the strict tradition, who interrupted my exposition from his chair and upbraided me with authority: "How can you say, not even as a joke, 'I am Brahma', when it is such an evident contradiction to try to equate a finite, and very finite and limited being indeed, with the infinitude of God?" I answered: "I also say every morning with faith and reverence 'This is my Body', and I understand that what to an indifferent observer may appear to be an absurd proposition between two mutually irreconcilable terms, is to me, in the gratitude of the accepted gift, source of grace and salvific mystery. Let us extend to other religions the respect we also want from them." Two things happened then simultaneously in the large hall where the academic function was being held. The president got up furious and tried to say something; and at the same time the entire hall resounded with a noisy ovation from the clapping of my fellow students, which drowned his remarks and saved my life. Later I came to know that the president had sent to Rome with something less than friendly intentions a detailed report of my public utterances on that day (without informing me), and that my name came back absolved from any suspicion of heresy. The inquisitorial fires were not lit.

That way is not, of course, the most popular, but it is

considered the noblest and purest and worthiest both of God and of man. Avoiding pantheistic extremes, this is the way of the mystics, whatever their language or non-language may be, and they keep up, in all latitudes and all religious climates, the sacred fire of God's inaccesibility together with his ineffable union with man. This concept of God is difficult, even dangerous, but healthy and necessary to safeguard his infinitude; or rather, it is a non-concept which gives up everything to gain everything. This concept has nursed, more than any other, the seeds of contemplation and adoration in the heart of man. The only thing is, one cannot sing carols to such a God.

There is still a third model in Hinduism. The God of action. The practical dogma of duty for duty's sake, the commandment of doing good and honouring life, thus entering into the cosmic cycle of successive reincarnations, each of which is determined by the deeds of the previous one in ascending rhythm towards the final liberation and eternal bliss. Here one reaches God, not through devotion or contemplation, but through action, through work, through duty; and consequently God becomes the order of the universe, the moral equilibrium that rewards good and punishes evil, the law of inner behavioural coherence between all that exists. To know is to act, work is prayer, and orthopraxis rules orthodoxy. This looks very abstract, but it was on this philosophy of the way of action that Gandhiji based his independence programme; and the Indian people, who know the doctrine because they live the tradition, understood him at once..., and the British empire had to relinquish "the jewel on the crown". The "way of action" can turn out to be eminently practical.

The particular and deep interest of Hinduism lies in the coexistence and the official recognition of the three models,

64

the practical option this gives to each group or individual, and even to the same person in different stages of his spiritual ascent; and finally the interaction of the three models among themselves in the history of India and in the heart and mind of every Hindu. In India there is no suspicion of the mystic (the West cannot say the same), and no looking down on the simple devout soul; the highest philosophy can go hand in hand with the humblest piety, and out of that secular cooperation grows the many-sided richness of the Hinduism of today and always, of sages and saints, of depth and popularity, of transcendent experience in the sacred triangle that form both the geography and the philosophy of eternal India.

I leave without answering the question, What would have happened if Jesus had been born in India? because I know it has no answer. That was no obstacle to my enjoying fully, if not gastronomically certainly intellectually, my breakfasts with the great thinker and master that was Kakasaheb Kalelkar.

ABORIGINAL RICHES

India is known for all the great world religions that have
found a home in it, but is less known for other religions,
varied and ancestral, which are followed by immense
multitudes and have much to contribute to the religious and
cultural heritage of mankind. They are the aboriginal
religions. Original and independent in themselves, colourful
in their traditions and their beliefs, rich in their folklore and
their festivals, they subsist with unspoilt vigour in the virgin
India of the tribes and the villages, in the plains and in the
forests of the generous geography of the whole subcontinent. They make up the animistic tradition which unites
India with black Africa, as Islam unites her with the Arab
world, Buddhism with the rest of Asia, and Christianity with
Europe. India at the centre of spiritual crossroads.

The aboriginal lives very close to nature, and from it he
derives his strength. Nature for him is "animated", full of
soul, full of life; his God is heaven and earth with all they
contain in trees and animals and flowers and rains, all
enriched with a variegated mythology of creations and
deluges and titanic fights between the forces of good and

evil, all lived in the free open liturgy of the long festivals where vast regions converge for the celebration of the life of the people who live closest to it. To begin to understand them one has to see them dance.

The dance is a religious activity. In India we say that God creates the universe by dancing. He does not "create" the world, but "dances" it into existence. And then, in inevitable cycle, he destroys it by dancing. There is much theology in that. The dance is not distinct from the dancer, and yet it does add something to the Creator's bare existence, since a still dancer is not the same as a dancing dancer. One image is worth many dogmas. That is why the whole of India loves dancing, and each region has its style, and each group its tradition.

There are no dancing schools among the aborigines. They learn how to dance as they learn how to live, and they practice their steps as they move, as they walk, as they work with the rhythm they carry in their bodies and show spontaneously in every graceful move. While I am teaching my mathematics class in the university, I often see through the window a group of aboriginal women who walk through the street on their way to work. They go singing and dancing in the midst of the traffic of the modern city, bold stroke of life over a canvas of steel.

I have just mentioned that they go to work, and that is the only thing they heartily dislike. I am convinced God never meant the aborigines to work. They do it only when they cannot help it because they need to earn something if they are to subsist; but they leave it at once as soon as they have something in their pockets to manage for a while. Productivity and saving are not concepts in their culture. One day in the morning I saw a woman sitting on the footpath

68

and selling the freshly cut thin branches of the lemon tree which most Indians use to brush their teeth with in the morning instead of a toothbrush. It is not to their taste, and it goes against their idea of cleanliness, to put into their mouths a repeated piece of plastic day by day, and they prefer the vegetable touch of the fresh branch whose end they bite first to make it into a brush, and whose sap they suck out to act as toothpaste, to rub it thoroughly in the slow morning ritual, and to discard it after use in the popular luxury that permits them to use a new toothbrush each day. That is why they have also to be bought each day, and that was the humble business of that humble woman on the footpath. That day business had been swift, and the whole stock had been disposed of early. I noticed it and told her, a slave myself still to the Western mentality of activity, productivity and competition that never quite leaves me even after having lived so many years in India: "You have still time to bring another load, and could earn double today." She looked at me uncomprehendingly, collected her scanty belongings and murmured while going: "Earn double? Why? Today I have already today's earnings; and tomorrow's earnings will come tomorrow." A new market economy. I would like to hear Galbraith on it.

The aboriginal has no sense of sin or moral guilt. I learned that at my own cost one year during Holy Week celebrations. I had gone for those holy days to a remote village in deep aboriginal country where a priest friend of mine had opened a new field and was working in it with great zeal. He asked me for a favour. There were in his parish about twenty adults who had accepted Jesus and had been baptized a few months before. They already led a full sacramental life, but they had not yet made their first confession, and the arrival of a priest from outside like myself, what is technically called an "extraordinary confessor", seemed the appropriate occasion for their first sacramental confession, as it would avoid the natural shame to have to mention their own sins to the parish priest they daily dealt with. He assured me he had instructed them well, and I had only to exercise my priestly ministry with those new penitents in their first reconciliation experience. I agreed immediately. I prepared a room with a homely atmosphere, and waited for my first penitent. He came in. He was a tall healthy lad, upright and composed. He walked up to me, touched with the fingers of both hands the crucifix that lay on my table, then touched his own forehead with the same fingers, stood erect and waited. I made him sit down, put him at ease, then said a little prayer with him, and waited. They were well instructed and they knew what they had to do. But this one was not starting. I had to do the starting. I felt my way with great tact and delicacy. "Now that we have prayed together before God, and we are in his sacrament of reconciliation, where I as a priest represent him for his pardon and blessing, would you like to mention some wrong you have done, for God to forgive you?" He interrupted me, and said in a tone of genuine surprise: "Who, I? Some wrong? No, Father, never; I don't do any wrong." Good beginning. I tried again with clearer words. "Any sin you may have committed...?" He almost bolted: "Sin? That I have sinned? Please, Father, don't say such things. I never do harm to anybody." And that was that. There was no way of getting a "confession" out of him. And the parish priest had assured me they all had been thoroughly instructed! I wondered what would have happened if they had not been! I finished the sacrament as well as I could, and called the next man. Same experience. And so with each one of them. There was no luck. I drew a blank each time. Out of twenty neophytes I did not get a single sin. What I did get was the sad reflection that

70

disturbed my mind: Could it be that Christianity consists in making us feel sinners first so that we may later feel redeemed? Those young men were honest people, healthy and straight, who, no doubt, had their own defects and failures, but for whom the idea of "offending God" was simply inconceivable. It did not enter their minds. They did understand, and that was their great and sole commandment, that no harm should be done to anybody; but even that was not for them a moral evil for which one had to repent, but just a damage that had been caused and which had to be made up for by paying for the expenses, and that was all. And to think that I had studied canon law and moral theology for two years only for that! I left those hefty lads to their parish priest, wondering whether he could finally teach them how to sin properly... so that they could make good confessions.

The great dark shadow over the aboriginal world is the practice of black magic. Sorcerers, magicians, witch doctors exploit the common people's credulity and work on their fears. The concept of God in nature leads to occult forces, charms, spells and curses, and from there to the elementary fear of man before nature, and to its abuse at the hands of those who know how to manipulate that fear and exploit it for their own gains.

The great opportunity and the great challenge for the millions of aborigines in India today is to keep their identity in the midst of other currents that want to assimilate them, to protect themselves against vested interests that seek to dominate them, and against the very material progress that is invading everything; and still to keep their candour, their charm and innocence to refresh and redeem this complicated world we live in.

71

JOKES AND TERRORISM

They are set apart by their turban, their beard neatly
collected in a hairnet, and the steel bracelet on their wrist.
Even without knowing his name any of them can be
addressed by the name "sardarji", which means "captain",
and will answer at once with a winning smile. Any of them
can also be addressed as "Mister Singh", which means
"Mister Lion", and will also readily answer, as all of them
add the denomination "Lion" at the end of their surnames.
They are capable businessmen who dominate commerce in
North India, and distinguish themselves in many academic
and managerial professions (one of them is the brightest of
all my mathematical friends); still, a mixture of natural
goodness and proverbial naivete makes them the loving butt
of special jokes, and so we have sardarji jokes in India as
they have "Scottish jokes" in England and "Polish jokes" in
the United States. When someone tells one, someone else is
sure to follow with another and still another, till someone in
the group calls for everybody's attention and says: "Have
you heard the joke of the intelligent sardarji?" They keep
quiet, and he begins: "There was once an intelligent
sardarji...". And in the ensuing suspense he declares: "That

73

was the joke." If a *sardarji* is in the group, he will be the first to laugh heartily.

The *sardarjis* are the *Sikhs*. Historically they are a people of peace, who sook harmony between the two great Indian religious communities, Hindus and Muslims, and tried to reconcile their religious beliefs in a new creed with traits derived from both; and as peaceful people they continue to live. But history has, ironically and sadly, led them along other paths, and a people, born and made for peace, fought first against the Mohammedans, then against the British, and now against humanity in that tragic gesture of barren separatism that has branded with fire and iron the hapless society of our days.

Some chapters ago I have spoken of the manipulation God suffers at the hands of politicians. This is one more sad example in the list. There is a racial, linguistic, historical, religious unity between a noble people in a large country. In that soil grows the ambition of a few, the temptation to the power they will acquire in a state of their own, the dreams of new prosperity in a separate land... and separatism is born. Political ambition takes cover under religious fervour. We have to safeguard the purity of our religion, we have to die for our faith, we have to defend God. That is, we have to kill in the name of God. And a temple becomes an arsenal, sermons become harangues, religion becomes politics, and love becomes hatred. Religious terrorism, unfortunate plague of our age in many peoples and distant countries, is the ultimate degradation of misused religion.

The Sikh religion was shaped under ten gurus in unbroken succession, and that strong leadership gave it energy and cohesion, but it also created a dangerous dependence on the guru's personality. Aware of that danger the last

74

guru, Govind Singh, suppressed the institution, declared that there would be no more gurus, and established in their place the Holy Book, the Granth Sahib, that would henceforth rule with its presence the destinies of its people. This is the Holy Book kept in the Golden Temple at Amritsar, and which, not only by its contents and doctrine, but by its very physical reality and sacramental presence, is the centre of the faith and devotion of the Sikh people. There is something very beautiful in that consecration and fidelity to the unique written witness of God's presence on earth, incarnation of his real presence and his living word. But there is a danger also in projecting God's concept onto a single book, however noble its origin and exalted its doctrine, because the book asks for a showcase, a showcase requires a temple, a temple a territory, and the territory requires an authority which becomes at one time religious and military, and will claim in its day separation and political sovereignty for the territory which the Book presides over. To limit the concept of God in time and space to a temple and a land, leads in the long run to "religious" war and "sacred" terrorism. That is why Indira Gandhi was murdered.

We had had enough suffering in India with the permanently latent friction between Hindus and Mohammedans for the Sikhs to add a new front to religious friction. I was once in Nice attending an international mathematical congress with India's delegation in which was also the Sikh colleague I mentioned at the beginning of the chapter. We were commenting on the true brotherhood that prevails in the world scientific community, and which manifested itself clearly in that congress where Russians and Americans, Christians and Hindus, believers and atheists mixed freely with one another without barriers of any kind, learning from each other in full mathematical fellowship

75

above all prejudices and frontiers. He was as religious a person as he was intelligent, and, when sharing experiences, though the Sikh problem did not then have the importance and the urgency it was soon to acquire, he could not help making a painful commentary: "It would seem as though science unites us, while religion divides us." The paper he read in the congress won wide acceptance, and was followed by a lively discussion among those present. It would not then have occurred to him that a different experience awaited him one day in his own country and in his own university. In the sad days that followed the murder of Indira Gandhi by her personal Sikh guard, my colleague, when he went to give his daily class, known and appreciated for the brilliance of his expositions and the swiftness of his arguments, found the hall empty, and the blackboard on which he wrote his equations full of the foul language of base insult. The blood, shed in Delhi, had stained his classroom, and the crime of his brothers in religion had darkened for a time the brightness of his demonstrations.

Violence, separatism and terrorism have sadly blurred the image, till now always charming and kind, of the turban and the beard in its net and the steel bracelet on the wrist. We do not tell any more "sardarji jokes" in India. It is a great pity.

THE EMPTY MIND

The first time a Hindu, speaking about prayer, asked me, "Father how to still the mind, avoid thought and fight distractions so that the mind might be perfectly empty in contemplation?", I answered with the impulsive tone of aggressive self-sufficiency: "Prayer does not consist in emptying the mind, but, on the contrary, in filling it up; filling it with good thoughts, holy resolutions, words of God in Scripture, of our own reflections on them, and of whatever the Lord may tell us in prayer, and we tell him. An empty mind is no use whatever; it has to be filled by God, and that is what prayer is for." I felt quite proud about my answer which embodied in its fullness my conceited Western superiority of spiritual colonizer to the pagan world, and I felt sure I had given that person a good lesson in the art of prayer. It is also true that already then I noticed in the attitude of my interrogator, a distinguished lady of exquisite manners in the highest circles of Bombay, that there was something in my answer that had jarred on her, though she promptly covered up the momentary embarrassment by deftly changing the subject of conversation. I felt ill at ease, made a mental note of my slip, whatever that was, and waited for life in India to bring me the answer as in so many of my initial bewilderments. In fact it took me years to discover and understand and appreciate the Orient's manner of prayer, and the difference, typical and fundamental to all East-West differences, in understanding the religious reality of man and his way of reacting to life and endeavouring to draw near to God. All that is reflected and expressed in the different approaches to prayer, and all this again reflects and influences the differences in the concept of God.

We could almost say in quick summary that the fundamental religious, theological, ascetical difference between East and West is that the West wants to fill the mind, while the East wants to empty it. In my formal religious training I was taught that the meditation had to be "practical", that it had to be carefully prepared with "points" painstakingly worked out the previous night, with foreseen considerations and directed dialogues (coloquies) with Our Lord. In my novitiate they told the story of the novice who dared, with sacrilegious but unavoidable gesture, to interrupt the morning prayer of a companion in order to ask him which was the second point of the meditation proposed the previous night by Father Master, since he could not remember it, and could not proceed or go back for the life of him in a pitiful contemplative impasse. And, above all, from the meditation one had to "draw fruit" each day, its influence had to be felt if it had to be genuine. What have you meditated about today?, How did you fare?, What fruit have you obtained? were questions one should be prepared to answer after an hour of prayer. Our good Father Master liked to repeat to us, perhaps even a little too often: "You get up early in the morning, you prepare your prayer, you spend a whole hour on your knees..., and if after all that you do 'nothing' in that hour, you get 'nothing' out of it, you change 'nothing' in your life as a result of it... well, my dear novices, you are wasting your time."

All these concepts, however legitimate they may be and however useful they may seem to us, are pure heresy in the East. Apart from the notion of "wasting one's time", which is exclusively and tormentingly a Western notion, the idea of "getting" something out of contemplation, of applying managerial standards to the activity of the spirit, of seeking "productivity" as in world markets, and so to set up a goal and measure results, all that, I say, would destroy for the Oriental mind the very essence of meditating in peace. The Oriental wants to contemplate reality, to be one with oneself in unity of mind and senses, of soul and body, of person and environment, a unity which gives back its balance to the soul and its well-being to the whole person, through which one finds God in the silence of the senses and the oneness of being. We have to still the noise of the mad traffic of living, and the greatest noise is not that of the city outside but that of the world inside, not that of the ears but that of the intellect, and that is why we have to stop ideas, silence thought, empty the mind.

The "prayer of quiet" is not exclusive to the East, but is known and practiced by contemplatives and mystics in every religion and in all climates. The difference is that in the West that kind of prayer has been traditionally minimized, avoided, even suspected of not squaring with true orthodoxy. "Quietism" is a condemned heresy, and "illuminism" illuminated many bonfires for the Inquisition. The apparent passivity of mystical waiting never quite fitted into the practical and active mentality of the Western way of life. And yet in the Orient that attitude is obvious, connatural and evident; and hence came the spontaneous question. How to empty

79

the mind? which I, in my Indian beginnings, did not know how to answer.

To empty the mind one has to go on reducing little by little the intellectual content of one's prayer. A universally popular method in India is the simple repetition of God's name. United to nature's rhythms of the breathing of the body, the beating of the heart or the falling of the steps while walking, it can become a deep and fruitful prayer that keeps the contact without burdening the mind. It is enough to travel in India in any train compartment, preferably a second class which will always be full to capacity, and observe unobtrusively the lips of one's travelling companions, to realize how general and natural this powerful prayer is in India. I do not idealize Indian landscapes, and do not say that everybody in every journey is praying all the time. There are travellers who smoke or sleep or read the paper or play cards. But there in that corner sits a man of mature age who is not reading the paper nor chatting nor smoking. Only his lips are moving imperceptibly in rhythmical silence. He is travelling with God. And on the other side there is a young mother with a child in her arms whom she looks at, speaks to, gently caresses... while her lips also caress the name of God. The sacred name, the loving repetition, the ceaseless prayer, the vital contact. The whole of India breathes God's name in the winds of the Himalayas and the waves of the Ganges, in the pilgrimages of her peoples and in the singing of her temple bells, in the breath of her faithful and the movement of their lips. A whole continent's heart beating to the name of God, and doing it so quietly, so simply and naturally that it is hardly noticed, hardly paid attention or given importance to, which is the highest nobility of man's prayer ever.

One day, very early in the morning, in the cold of Mount

Abu in the heart of Rajasthan's winter, I was walking the
distance of a little over a kilometer that separated our house
from the convent of Sisters where I was to say their community Mass. The road was deserted, I was well wrapped up
in a thick sweater, muffler and gloves, and was walking fast
to react against the morning cold. The solitary walk was part
of the hour of meditation I had to put in in the morning as a
preparation for the Eucharist I was going to celebrate; but
there was nothing to prevent me from looking around as I
walked and noticing the surroundings. After a while I noticed that someone else was walking on the same empty road
ahead of me. It was a small woman, dressed in a scanty
saree tucked up between her legs as is usual with working
women who need to move more freely. On her head she
carried an enormous load of firewood, which she balanced
with a long pole fixed to the rear of the bundle and deftly
manipulated by her right hand. Her steps were small but
swift, she was barefooted, and the cloud of her breath and
the frailness of her figure created a painful blurr of human
cold on the ruthless landscape. I knew there were poor
families around who earned a meager livelihood out of
collecting the dry fallen branches of mountain trees, and
selling them at the break of day in the central market. That
was where the little woman was going when I saw her. I was
walking faster, drew level with her, and overtook her. While
doing so I noticed she was muttering something, and I paid
attention without slowing my step. To the rhythm of her
bare feet on the frozen asphalt she was repeating with stub-
born and tender devotion the sacred words: "Oh my God;
oh my Lord! Oh my God; oh my Lord!" She was praying
while walking, her steps were the beads of her rosary, her
theology was made up of two words, God and Lord, and
her faith and devotion filled the whole silent dawn over the
golden peaks. I heard her brief ejaculatory prayer grow

81

fainter and fainter as I moved ahead. Only now I was moving with something to think about. There was I, wrapped up in my muffler, making my morning "meditation", that is, thinking of the great breakfast the good sisters were going to give me after the Mass—that rich fare was the great attraction of those morning visits to the convent, since breakfast in our own house was a sadly masculine and desperately monotonous affair. That was a fine meditation I was making! Theological training, long studies, thousands of hours of meditation, priesthood, vows, retreats and recollections...., and that little village woman was praying better than I was; rather, she was praying and I was not. And she was praying because she had at hand the simple way of doing it, because she had inherited an ancestral reflex that made her pronounce God's name spontaneously when walking, when breathing, when living, as part and parcel of her own being. Prayer, when it becomes truly simple, grows by itself and fills everything. I had quite a bit of thinking to do that winter morning up the empty road to the convent. When I arrived, at the Eucharist, after reading the Gospel and starting to make some reflections, I put aside the thoughts I had prepared the previous day, and plainly and simply told my experience. It was a far better sermon.

There are also abuses. A famous one, because the historical fact was written into a play and taken to the stage from where it scandalized a whole generation, was about a mother-in-law who, while preparing the poison that killed her daughter-in-law did so repeating God's name out of ingrained habit, and so for a criminal instant, she converted worship into sacrilege. There is of course routine and forgetfulness and manipulation and all the thousand and one miseries human beings will invent to undo and spoil the holiest of customs. But the fundamental principle stands.

82

Reduce the intellectual content of your prayer, and its quality will improve. Silence the mind, and the heart will speak.

This is only the gateway from which new roads and paths lead to more and more refined teachings and practices to still the mind and awaken faith. There are many schools and multiple experiences; but the direction is one and constant. Disown the appearances to assert reality, tame thought to liberate truth, empty the mind to let God fill it. That has been India's business for centuries untold. True, there is also in India, and tourism and news media take it upon themselves to display its images all through the world, the parallel cult of the "God of devotion" with its noisy and multitudinous manifestations; the many-coloured show-window which attracts the superficial looks of the merely curious to the easy folklore, and thus protects and keeps safe the family secret from the casual inquirer; the outside cover, which for many remains only a cover, of the mystical treatise of wisdom and experience which teaches how to reach God. All that lives side by side in India, and throbs and interacts and thrills and vivifies. And in the centre of it all remains always the supreme non-image of the God without a face and without a name because his name is above all names and his concept beyond all concepts. India's great prayer is silence, because India's greatest concept of God is the God of negation. That is why the mind had to be emptied.

83

TRADE WITH THIS WHILE I AM AWAY

It is not easy to empty the mind. It is not easy to silence thought. It is not easy to dismiss the image. I want to underline the practical difficulty of departing from the known and changing approaches in religious behaviour, by telling an incident that took place in this same "land of negation", the sacred India that occupies my thoughts.

To fight the evils of superstition among simple people, a progressive group of young Hindus hit on the idea of themselves going from village to village as a company of actors to stage plays they themselves had composed, and which, together with witty dialogue and entertaining scenes, carried a clear and definite message against superstition, blind faith and all kind of abuses committed in the name of religion.

One of their plays had the following argument. The makeshift stage was set up in the centre of the main square in the village at night when the villagers had finished their labours and their supper, and the general curiosity, as yet unspoilt by the slavery of television, took over at the hour of leisure and brought everybody to the central square. The young actors discussed the so-called miracles performed by the *sadhus*, the holy men venerated throughout India as men of God, some of whom take advantage of the credulity of the masses to earn both respect and money with magic tricks, which in fact are mere sleight of hand, but are made to appear as religious feats. A favourite one is to make holy ashes, which are the object of special veneration, appear in the closed fist which a moment before was shown to be open and empty, and then make as though those ashes came out of the neck or the sleeve of any willing victim, or even make ashes rain from the air to the surprise and veneration of the credulous crowd. Also, holy pictures and medals of favourite gods and goddesses are made to appear, the sadhu may appear to be suspended in mid-air, he may tell events which occurred in the village during the past year and predict those which are going to occur in the new. A fairly complete programme that repeats itself from feast to feast and from village to village, with a few local and personal touches; a performance which helps to satisfy the spiritual needs of the village and the material needs of the sadhu. In India one has only to put on saffron not to go hungry.

Our young actors discussed all this on the stage, and then, as part of the show itself, they made a public offer to the audience: "If there is any sadhu among you who is ready to perform any of these miracles here on the stage before everybody, we will give him a million rupees." That offer shook the audience more than the dramatic finale of the greatest stage thriller. The million rupees were duly exhibited, and that was more money and more banknotes than any in the village had ever seen or dreamt of seeing in his whole life, and the suspense of the bold challenge took hold of the village for a few intense moments. All necks turned this way and the other, all villagers longingly hoped that a

86

champion of the faith would appear, and those shameless young actors would lose the million rupees.

Then came out the champion of the faith. Right from behind the audience rung the cry "Jay Mahadev!", battle-cry of spiritual combat, something like "Praise the Lord!" against the attacks of unbelief and the wiles of the devil; and a real sadhu, complete with long beard, sacred trident and saffron garb, stood up in the last row, bold and sure of himself, advanced slowly through the cheering audience, climbed the stage, invoked the name of God, and proceeded to perform all the standard miracles as expected by the people and derided by the actors. The ashes, the medals, the pictures and the prophecies, with a couple of extra items thrown in. The sadhu, of course, was one of our young actors properly disguised, though the audience did not know or even suspect it, and thought him to be a genuine man of God and his miracles also genuine. After his flawless performance, the audience demanded that he should be given the million rupees, and the rationalistic actors, in full discomfiture, had to grant the popular demand.

At that moment another actor came up from within the audience, introduced himself as an agnostic and a magician, and went on to repeat one by one all the sadhu's tricks explaining how they worked and showing that there was nothing miraculous in them. Faced with that evidence even the sadhu had to yield, and he confessed before everybody that he had cheated the people; with that he asked for pardon and returned the million rupees. That was not yet the end, since, to imprint the lesson deeper in the mind of the people, the actors then grew indignant, pounced on the sadhu and proceeded to beat him lustily. The beating was only a stage illusion, of course, without real blows, but it was sufficiently well practised to appear real and make the sadhu

87

ask for mercy while jumping over the whole stage to avert the blows.

And here comes the interesting point which was repeated again and again in every village and before every audience without fail; and that is the point of my story. The people perfectly understood that the so-called sadhu was an impostor, and that the whole thing was mere stage play; but such was the power of the "cloth", the saffron colour, the image of the man of God in the minds of the people that, when the beating began, the spectators rose to a man, and started shouting, "Don't beat him! Leave him alone! Let him go! He is a man of God! Don't do him any harm!" And the rationalistic actors, for all their reforming zeal, saw their evidence destroyed by the religious feeling of a devout people. They managed to get their million rupees back, but there was no beating, there was no lesson.

The people were no fools. They knew perfectly well what had happened. But the image never dies, and to see a man who is dressed in religious garb, even if he is an actor, get a beating, even a mock beating, is something the village public cannot bear. The image hurts, jars, disturbs. The public sides with the saffron and shouts with one voice: "Leave him alone!"

The image never dies. It does not die in us either. We accept the transcendence, we recognize the mystery, we respect the silence. But the image persists and the concept holds on and the idea refuses to quit. There is deep within us, at the very fringe of our consciousness, a mixture of routine, laziness, fear, superstition, resistance to change and acquiescence with familiarity that holds on desperately to initial values, repeats attitudes and projects childhood images onto the rest of our lives. The family album to which we lovingly go back again and again, because it guarantees that our present is the continuation of our past. The danger is that continuity may mean stagnation.

There is an expression in Spanish which has an undoubted religious value, but which I also consider dangerous for the frequency, the circumstances and the very candour with which it is profferred. The expression is "the coalman's faith". It takes the image of a humble profession, the worker who covers himself with black dust when carrying on his shoulders the sacks of coal from coal cellar to coal cellar; it supposes that the worker has no studies and much faith, that he is happy with his life and thanks God for it without complaining or asking why he has to carry with labour the coal others will burn for their comfort; and so sets him up as a model before a sophisticated society which smothers the concept of God under the burden of philosophical doubts and existential complaints, darker in their souls than the dust on the coalman's hands. The phrase is made, and honest intellectual Catholics are heard to proclaim with pride: "My faith is the coalman's faith!"

During a trip to Spain I was once talking with a very well-read lady, and the conversation, due to my religious character and to my ignorance of topical themes of which my absence from Spain had kept me in the dark, inevitably turned to religious themes. I tentatively mentioned the name of some modern theological movement, when the learned lady stopped me dead and said: "I don't want to hear anything of these modern religious ideas. For me it is and it has always been... the coalman's faith." Maybe it was because I was hearing that phrase for the first time in many years, or because of the marked contrast between the elegant lady and a coalman, or again because of my personal interest in making a hobby out of advances in exegesis,

Christology or any serious religious thought, but the fact is I reacted quickly and sharply and said something like this: "You are a very intelligent and learned person, much above an ordinary cultural level; you know a good deal about art and music, can distinguish at first sight between a Renoir and a Monet, you speak five languages, you can tell me the latest Goncourt prize or the latest Nadal; you have told me that you prefer Ricardo Mutti to Claudio Abbado as an orchestra conductor, and you can hold intelligently and interestingly a conversation about almost any topic in the world... except religion. Something has gone wrong there. You have increased your knowledge and refined your tastes in all directions... except one, which is your understanding of God and Christ and his Gospel. In the matter of religion you go only by the catechism you learned as a child and the Bible classes you attended at school God knows how many years ago. And there you got stuck. You know much about many things, and practically nothing about religion. You have developed all your faculties, except your religious understanding. And you take quick refuge, almost with pride, in the old saying, the coalman's faith. I understand the partial validity of that claim and I appreciate it, but to you I say now with blunt frankness: the coalman's faith, my dear and appreciated lady, is for the coalman, just as the engineer's faith is for the engineer, the philosopher's faith for the philosopher, and the intellectual's for the intellectual. The trouble with Catholic society today is that the older generation among us has not developed an intelligent understanding of Christianity parallel to the understanding of their profession and cultural environment. We have great technicians, doctors, engineers, economists and managers who are authorities in their respective fields, knowledgeable in all common topics... and coalmen in religion. That's how we have fared." The elegant lady withstood my tirade, and came graciously out of the embarrassment telling me with a smile: "You know, I'm mortally afraid of young priests like you." I was flattered to hear myself referred to as "young priest" when I am over sixty (though she was obviously more, which explains the relative term), and we parted friends. Maybe she forgot the incident; but for my part I sharply remembered the repartee that had come spontaneously to me in the heat of the exchange: the coalman's faith is all right... for the coalman!

The answer, besides, was not mine. It is in the Gospel. In it there is the story of a king who went to a far country, and left one of his subjects ten "talents", another subject, five, and still another, one, with the same injunction to each: "Trade with this while I am away." What are those "talents"? The word "talent" in English, probably a derivative from that Biblical root, has come to mean the skill or ability to do anything from music to computing. Everything has to be developed because everything comes from God. But there is no doubt that together with those talents of human coinage we have also been given and have to develop other "talents" of divine value, a more precious capital than physical strength or artistic value, gifts of virtue and of grace, of loving the neighbour and serving God, of prayer and of faith, of understanding moral doctrines and spiritual truths, of deepening religious teaching and enlarging catechism into theology, and simple understanding into enlightened knowledge; and above all we have been given the gift of the concept and understanding of God, gift of gifts, and consequently now responsiblity of responsibilities. That is the original "talent", gold coin with God's name engraved on it, pledge and guarantee of all other talents of mind, body and soul; divine talent which now has to be invested, multiplied, developed, put to bear fruit while the

91

King "is away". We have to enlarge the concept of God which was given us when we started life, we have to enrich the concept, we have to make full use of the talent which represents and bears in itself all other talents.

One of the king's subjects took the talent, wrapped it in a piece of cloth, buried it in his garden, and when the king came back he took it out, untied it, cleaned it, polished it and produced it triumphantly before the king: "Here is your talent! Just as you gave it to me." And the king got angry.

So I think that if anyone keeps that talent of talents, the talent of the concept of God, exactly and literally as it was given him at the beginning of his conscious life, if he is afraid, suspicious, distrustful, however faithful and loyal he may profess himself to be, and goes and digs and hides the talent; and when he meets the King again he digs out the talent and proffers it, polished but solitary, and tells him: "Lord, here is the talent you gave me; the concept to be had of you in my own mind, greatest treasure and love of all my life. Here it is exactly as you gave it to me, the same in weight and measure, without stain or notch; the same concept that my godfather had of you when he recited for me the creed at my baptism; the concept I learned in my catechism and professed in my first communion, the concept I have defended against temptations and doubts and novelties, and which now I present before you, pure and shining, with the exactness of my care and the witness of my vigilance."…, I think, I say, that if anyone thinks that way and acts that way, and believes that by doing so he will receive congratulations and benefits at the end of the journey, he will be sorely disappointed when he stands up and looks up and sees the face of the King and hears his verdict. The King will get angry.

"Trade with this while I am away." We have to trade with the greatest treasure we possess: The very concept of God. We have to advance in his knowledge.

COME AND SEE

When I say concept I mean experience. There is no question here of abstract concepts, but of living experience. Or rather, there is question of everything together, since in practice ideas shape behaviour, and behaviour influences ideas. In Biblical language "to know" a person means to deal with him, so much so that for a man "to know" a woman means having a sexual relationship with her. The concept we have of a person is born and takes shape in the personal dealings we have with him or her in the family and in society. Our concept of God is inseparable from our experience of God.

For many long years, in spite of the trust and intimacy that characterized my dealings with Jesus as my personal friend, the "experience" of God was a forbidden expression for me. It smelled of presumption, mysticism, "singularity", and one of the greatest crimes one could commit in our cloister and in our time was that of being "singular". We all had to follow the trodden path, and no experiments or novelties were tolerated. Our good novice master seemed to enjoy repeating the old chauvinistic joke: "When you are

95

priests and any religious Sister comes to you and speaks of extraordinary communications she has from God, or says that she sees, hears, feels anything out of the ordinary, tell her Mother Superior to give her a good chunk of 'country ham' for breakfast, and that will be the end of all her mystical experiences." "Country ham" is Spain's speciality: freshly cured and thickly cut ham, tasty and full of calories, an apparently sure remedy against any kind of supernatural claims in prayer.

In India there is no "country ham". And in India I was engulfed with truly Pentecostal violence by the "charismatic movement" which created one of the greatest spiritual upheavals in my life. I must have been about fifty then and felt solid and proud (was that holy pride?) on the strength of my long theological formation, my ministry as a priest, my years of prayer, and my experience in directing many souls. But then came the storm and I was caught unawares. A companion gave me a book to read, David Wilkerson's "The Cross and the Switchblade", which was the slightly awkward but definitely real instrument of the charismatic revival that shook almost all the churches with the winds of Whitsunday. I read it three times with growing emotion. There was God acting in a tangible way through his Spirit in my own time and at my own door. Yet I resisted at the beginning. How could I, a man with the best religious formation in the world in the midst of the Catholic Church and of the Society of Jesus, priest and religious for so many years, orthodox Spaniard and missionary among pagans, how could I learn now something, and something radically and revolutionarily new, from a few American youngsters, Protestant into the bargain, who all of a sudden were unsettling the circumspection of my theology with the reality of their experiences? To hell with them! And yet what I read coincided

96

so much with what I wanted; the tangible action of the Holy Spirit in fervour and enthusiasm, in conversions and healings, in the gift of prophecy and discernment, was something so necessary and urgent for me, mere drop of Christianity in an ocean of indifference, that in the end I opened up, I yielded to the tide, and joy took hold of my life with supreme dominion over my whole existence. God, all of a sudden, had come alive to me.

The details of the story would distract us here, so I cut them out. I have told them in two articles I published in the movement's official magazine, "New Convenant", from Ann Arbor, Michigan in the United States, and then again, at the request of the editors of the same magazine, in a book made up of personal testimonies of charismatic experiences by people all over the world, which they themselves selected and edited. The book is called "Come and See", and one of its chapters is my story with my name and surname to it. In it is recorded the priceless experience which was going to seal my life with the seal of God's vision in all the reality and bliss which are humbly possible here below.

When speaking of God in India, there is a word which always unavoidably comes up: *darshan*. It means "vision", and it is used essentially of the vision of God... already in this life. Vision, contact, experience. That is the goal of all religious activities, the seal of authority to speak of God. He who has "seen" God has a right to speak about him, and he who has not, let him keep quiet. People broach the topic and, with the same ease with which they would ask, "Have you read Tagore?", they ask, "Have you seen God?" I used to be irritated by that question in my first years in India, and reacted sharply with Western arguments to the effect that what matters is faith, obscurity, the trust that we show God when we believe his word on his own authority, and the

97

attitude Jesus himself recommended in his answer to St. Thomas: "Blessed are those who believe without seeing!" My questioners listened politely to my answers, kept quiet and changed the topic. There was no *darshan*. I was not qualified. And my own irritation indirectly showed me that something hurt me there.

"Have you seen God?" was the question Narendra Dutt put to Shri Ramakrishna, who answered him in all simplicity: "Yes, and I can make you see him too." And so Narendra Dutt was transformed into Swami Vivekananda and founded the most important religious order in Hinduism, the Ramakrishna Mission, for the rules and constitutions of which he sought inspiration (history has its own ironies!) in the constitutions of the Society of Jesus. To see God was one of the three "madnesses" of Shri Aurobindo, the philosopher of Indian independence, metaphysical poet, and mystical leader, in life and after death, of spiritual inquirers in India and in the whole world. First madness: God exists. Second. If he exists, there must be a way to reach him, even in this life. Third: I am going to try and find this way with all my life. And there stands the material monument to his achievement in his *ashram* at Pondicherry, and the literary monument in his epic poem "Savitri". God, in India, is an experience, and, in the words of a Catholic monk, Bede Griffiths, who also has his own *ashram* in South India, "certainly in India we cannot expect the message of the Gospel to be accepted as a revelation from God, if it offers less to the devout Hindu than his own religion. The 'revelation' which God has given to India is a revelation of himself as the ground of being and the source of consciousness and the goal of absolute bliss. It is this experience of God which has to become the basis of an Indian Christian spirituality. For too long we have been content with a form of prayer which hardly goes beyond meditation and affective prayer; and the ancient ideal of contemplation, of the direct experience of God in prayer, has been almost lost to view. In the same way we have been content with a theology which is based on reason illumined by faith, but does not lead to an experience of God in the Spirit. It would seem that the Church in India is being challenged to recover the depth of her own spiritual tradition by contact with this Hindu tradition of the experience of God. An experience of God in the Spirit seems to be the great need of Christian spirituality today. The world is looking not for words about God, but for the experience of God. That is why so many, Christians and others, are coming to India to study Yoga and to learn meditation. The Church has to find an answer to this need for the experience of God, for the presence of the Spirit, and it is the Church in India, responding to the deepest intuition of the Indian soul, which should be able to give this answer." Important and authoritative quotation which reflects faithfully what every serious Christian thinks today in India.

When I came to India I was reminded of the general prohibition, in accordance with the vow and rules of poverty, to bring with us any book, however pious; and yet I consciously and flagrantly broke all the regulations and smuggled in with me the mystical contraband of the complete works of St. Teresa of Avila and St. John of the Cross. They form as much part of my spiritual make-up as the Exercises, Constitutions and correspondence of St. Ignatius Loyola. In later visits to Spain I went also to the convent of San Jose de Avila, where a copy of an interesting book is zealously kept. The book is the *"Tercer abecedario"* of Francisco de Osuna, the very copy St. Teresa used, and where she found definite help in her mystical ways. In that text, underlined in St.

Teresa's own hand is the following pithy and charming paragraph: "Friendship and intimacy with God is possible in this life we call exile; and that communication is not something of little volume, but it is closer and nearer and safer than there could ever be between brothers, or even between mother and son. If we call spiritual this friendship and communication of God to man, that does not mean it is not real and weighty with thruth and certainty. I speak of the communication sought and found by those persons who labour to achieve prayer and devotion, and which is so sure and certain that there is nothing surer in this world, and certainly nothing more joyful, valuable and delectable."

During one of those trips to Spain I went to see a play of the priest and playwright Martin Descalzo. The name of the play was "Two Sets of Cards", and it portrayed a priest's crisis in his vocation which he finally leaves (first act), and his new crisis, not smaller than the first, when he again makes up his mind and marries without success (second act). I went to the theatre with my mother, assuring her not to worry unnecessarily, as I was not going there to check on any personal doubts, but only to see a good play and to learn about reactions and pyschological situations. And, did I learn! The description of the growing doubt in the priest's soul was superb, as only a good priest and a good writer could have achieved. It held my interest from moment to moment, chiefly in the masterly dialogues between the priest and his bishop. One sentence of those dialogues stuck in my memory, and I have used it a hundred times in talks to priests and religious, and have always noticed that when I say it, a sudden and deep silence descends upon the hall and into the heart of all the listeners. The phrase is: "The crisis in the life of a priest begins the day he begins to ask himself the question: Was it worthwhile to give up so much... and to get so little?"

Accurate diagnosis brother priest and writer, accurate diagnosis! We may have given up much or little, but that was our "all" as the torn nets of Peter the fisherman were for him when he spoke of "all" he had given up to follow Jesus. And, what have we received in exchange? Eternal life. So we hope. But, what about some advance payment here below? If there is only official work, routine prayer, "life of faith" (in the respectful but dry sense of the term), repeated liturgies and affective loneliness... the conclusion "to get so little" becomes unavoidable, unbearable, and it weighs like a millstone on the life of the priest. The phrase hit me, that is, I was then in a psychological position where I could allow myself to be hit by it, without starting to put up false defences of personal pretension or pious resignation, precisely because at that moment in my life I was able to answer gloriously and triumphantly: "Yes, I have given up much, I have given up everything for Christ..., but I have received very much more than I have given! I have received the immeasurable joy, the supreme bliss, the direct presence, the irrefutable evidence of grace and glory and the truth of the Resurrection and the fullness of the Spirit; angels sing in my soul, and the whole of heaven vibrates in my senses. How well are we here, Lord, how well are we here in this replica of Mount Tabor, with or without a tent! Come and see, touch and feel. The Gospel is true, the Bible is real, the Resurrection is a fact and every Eucharist is a festival. My life has flowered into alleluias, and eternity has burst in my own hands. Blessed faith which is almost transcended down here by the anticipated realism of this rehearsal of heaven!"

Thus played the band, and the music was glorious. And it had to be. I had the whole of Scripture on my side. The God of Jesus was not, he said, a God of the dead but of the living; the Gospel is "news" (the Good News)... or it is nothing; the Christian is a witness, not a tape recorder; the "baptism of the Spirit" with all its sequel of joy and miracles and gift of tongues and apostolic expansion had recurred again and again in Jerusalem, Samaria, Damascus, Caesarea and Ephesus (all these are quotations from the Acts), and this last occasion was already twenty-five years after the first. Why should it stop there? That was how the Church has spread throughout the world, and that was how it had to spread now, if it were not to stagnate in its buildings and monuments and documents. The "power of the Resurrection" and the "power of the Spirit" are the two basic constants of the thrust of the Gospel, and they are as true today as they were then. Let us make way for that power in our lives, and the face of the earth will be renewed, which is the vivifying and creational work of the Spirit from the dawn of creation to this new Pentecost that has befallen us.

The charismatic revival gave rise to a sudden subculture of prayer meetings, songs, books, magazines, ways of speaking and styles of life which fostered the change and nourished the fervour. A favourite song of mine in those happy days was the Gospel song "The Present Tense" which summed up my experience and my joy.

> Your holy hearsay is not evidence;
> give me the goodnews in the present tense.
> What happened nineteen hundred years ago
> may not have happened... How am I to know?

> The living truth is what I long to see;
> I cannot lean on what used to be.
> So shut the Bible up and show me how
> the Christ you talk about is living NOW.

Those were years inebriatingly happy (which is the metaphor both Bible and liturgy use to describe the effects of the action of the Spirit), fully in the unexpected renewal that brought a new spring to the churches. The description is brief and falls far short of reality; I am fully aware of that, as I am of another fact too, which some attentive reader may have also noticed, namely that when speaking of all this experience of mine in the Pentecostal movement, I have spoken as of something past, something that once happened and is now over, that had a beginning and an end, that was a chapter in my life, important and influential, yes, but finished now and left behind while the story continues ahead. And that is the case. The experience came and went, and I consider it important to analyse its end as I have analysed its beginning, because in that contrast is embodied, with the anecdotal clarity of the concrete case, what is in fact theme and thesis of this book: the divine play of taking and leaving, coming and going, entering and departing. Let me explain that.

There were about seven years of this spiritual flood; and I do not say seven because it is a Biblical number, but because, collating memories, that is the approximate figure that comes out. And after that time I began somehow to notice that the flood was subsiding. I got alarmed. Was it my own negligence? I redoubled my prayers. But muscles do not work when the spirit fails. My alleluias were weaker and weaker, my part in prayer meetings more and more passive, and the latest issue of the magazine "New Covenant", which formerly I expected month after month as manna from heaven, now fell listlessly from my hands. My prayer companions noted my cooling down and prayed for me to recover my lost fervour. I longed for their prayers to be heard, but there was no trace of it. What was I to do?

Here comes what is for me one of the most interesting moments of my conscious life, and I intimately enjoy analys-

103

ing it and telling about it, which for me is again sign of its depth and genuinness. My first reaction when I saw my fervour diminish was to resist its coming down and to fight to bring it up again. Just as I had first resisted and refused to enter into the Pentecostal movement (or, more exactly, to allow it to enter me), so now I was resisting and refusing to leave it (or to allow it to leave me). I soon noticed the parallel, and that gave me light. If I had done well in letting it come, why should I not do well now letting it go? Why resist? Why hold on, why stick, why freeze? The Spirit is wind. Let him blow, let him come..., and let him pass on. To let him go is precisely the best way to make it easy for him to come again... when he wants and in the way he wants; while the sure way to lose him is to try to "possess" him. I do feel pain and even sorrow to have to take leave of these unearthly joys that have accompanied me all these years and which I thought would last for ever. But that too is greed, possessiveness, lack of trust. I cannot "possess" a wave in the sea. If I stick with a wave all that will happen is that it will throw me on the shore and will leave me there defenceless and alone; whereas if I let the wave pass, another and another will come, and they will keep rocking me with new rhythms in the eternal play of the ocean that speaks of God.

I had closed my first to hold on desperately to the precious experience of those blissful years so as not to allow it to escape. Now little by little I released my grip, loosened my fingers, opened my hand..., and let it go. Farewell, alleluias! The more I delved in self-examination, with all the faith and humility I could muster, the more I saw that the situation that had been complex and unclear for a start, became normal and beneficent as I let myself free to see it as it was. The intimate confirmation of the Spirit grew on me

104

with the joy of detachment, the renewed advance, the gratitude for past graces opening on to future ones, the interest of opening a new chapter in my story, and above all the evident satisfaction of having let God free. Today I feel happy to have allowed the charismatic movement to take hold of me when it came, and I feel happy to have allowed it to take leave of me when it went. It enriched me by coming, and it enriched me by going away. In those inner dynamics is where I see the essence of the charismatic movement, just as of any other movement, that is, in being a "movement", in coming and going, in entering and leaving; and when we want to freeze it we lose its strength. It is painful to get stuck in enthusiasm. I do not want to speak about others, though I have seen painful examples enough and to spare, but I speak of myself and say that if, out of what had been and remains a happy chapter in my biography, I would have wanted to make a whole biography, I would have spoilt the biography.

And that is, I say, what this book is driving at, very much in its own way, very much through bypaths and byways and personal memories and sketches of religions and parallel experiences: to say that we have to live with open windows, we have to let God come in and go out, enter and... leave if he pleases; that we have to make room in our minds for new ways of seeing and thinking, of praying and contemplating, of knowing and understanding God, without forcing anything, without ever doing violence to ourselves, be it in order to reject the new or to hold back the old; that we have to let God be God in his own way and in his own time, so that we may come to know more and more traits of his ever on-going incarnation.

Who said that if he did not go away, someone else (very important and very similar to him) would not come?

105

THE GOD OF OIL

According to Hilaire Belloc in his book "The Great Heresies" Islam is only a (heretical) sect of Christianity. The Koran knows and respects the Bible, and gives us Christians one of the most beautiful names we have ever been given: "The people of the Book." And would that we could make that brotherly Islamic blessing a reality in our lives! The Koran venerates Jesus as a prophet, and speaks deferentially of Mary, which gives me already a kind of family sense, of brotherhood, of closeness to the Islamic community. There is still the weight of the crusades and the image of St. James "the Moor-killer" (they say that whenever Arab dignitaries visited dictator Franco in his palace of El Pardo, he thoughtfully had the classical paintings that depicted St. James on his white horse driving the Moors out of Spain turned towards the wall), but the theological link is stronger for me than all historical clashes. In India, curiously, since both Christians and Mohammedans are minorities, we come together in mutual instinct of self-preservation, and readily help each other in all our problems. Our Catholic College is the one that has more Muslim students and professors in the whole state of Gujarat, and in sad times of violence between

Hindus and Muslims (to which I have already alluded) Mohammedan students have taken refuge in our own hostel.

It is in Islam that the commandment (which is the basis of this book) "you shall not make images of the Lord your God" has been most rigidly observed; but while the external observance has been zealously maintained, its inner spirit has been forgotten, and as a result the mental, conceptual, theological image of the God of Islam is the most monolithically unchangeable of all religions in the world. A Mohammedan scholar told me one day: "You Catholics are rigid enough, but at least you have popes and councils which can officially renew the interpretation of the Bible and open new paths in faith and morals; while we are permanently anchored in the Koran." It is refreshing to hear an impartial and spontaneous appreciation of the Catholic magisterium. What we used to call the "dogmatic progress" in our theology classes is no sterile scholastic thesis, but vital reality. The magisterium is not there only to protect the old but to encourage the new, not only to watch but to promote. It feels good to know that there are those who envy us for having it.

In reciprocal appreciation I venerate in Islam the total and unconditional submission of man to God's will as manifested in every instant and every event, big or small, of human history or of one's private life, of spirit or matter. God's creative act is an atomic action, that is, instantaneous, repeated, renewed at each moment, in such a way that the result that follows (let us say, the trajectory of a stone I have thrown) is not the "effect" that follows the "cause" (my throwing), but rather God creates at each instant a new situation with the stone a little farther on its way. The impression is that "I" threw the stone, but in reality the whole

108

action belonged to God alone. There are no "second causes", no human contingencies, no intermediate factors; only God and his will and his action. That basic concept of Islam, exposed here in an unavoidably inadequate summary, is no mere philosophical speculation, but a definite principle with concrete and practical consequences. I learned that one day in a friendly dialogue, though rather defensive on both sides, with an orthodox Mohammedan.

His argument, in a nutshell, was clear and radical: "God has given oil to the Arab countries; therefore Islam is the true religion." The argument, thus expressed, may look a little naive and hasty. The quick shift from petro-dollars to petro-dogma sounds rather crude (with a little play on words). That type of syllogism did not appear in the list of Aristotelian syllogisms we recited by heart in our logic class. And yet for that devout and learned Mohammedan the argument was unanswerable; and the same kind of petro-pride appears, with or without disguise, in the great Islamic revival our days are witnessing in culture and religion. The photographs of Arab sheiks discussing oil prices while fingering the beads of the Islamic rosary of God's holy names, have contributed to the modern image of Islam something similar (saving differences) to what television reports of pope John Paul II have contributed to present-day Catholicism Prestige, actualization, respect, influence. One image is worth a thousands words, and the image of the white burnouses and the Islamic rosaries in international conferences has strengthened Islam's position in the ecumenical forum of world religions today. Christianity has not been the only religion to profit from the communication media.

I have said that the oil argument was a consequence of the Islamic concept of God, and I now explain the proposition. God creates anew at every instant the total reality of

109

the universe we live in. Nature, therefore, if we know how to read it with eyes of faith, is the revelation of God's will written day by day for our instruction. That reading tells us that God has made coincide, both in history and in geography, the religion of his Prophet with the greatest reserves of crude oil when the world most needed it. The subsoil's essential riches proves the providential election of the people that lives on that soil. If humanity today needs oil, humanity needs Islam today. God's chosen people is the people favoured with a land that responds to the needs of today's world; and just as in other times the land of another chosen people flowed with milk and honey in an agricultural society, so now it flows with crude oil in an industrial society. The sign has changed with the times.

Since all the main religions are practised in India today, ecumenical meetings are common at all levels in an effort to foster mutual understanding and peaceful coexistence, and there is even a long and twisted word, to which Gandhiji himself gave currency, something like "all-religions-fellow-feeling", which is constantly used in such contexts and functions. On such occasions a Hindu speaks on Hinduism, a Mohammedan on Islam, a Jain on Jainism, a Sikh on Sikhism, a Parsi on Zoroastrianism, and a Christian on Christianity, while a patient audience listens to the ecumenical marathon, claps hands and bows heads in unison, sings out of tune some neutral psalmody, and comes out with the satisfaction of having fulfilled the duty that responsible citizens and good neighbours have to put up with everybody without understanding anybody. I used to accept with enthusiasm invitations to speak in such meetings on behalf of Christianity, as I saw in them a splendid opportunity to speak about Jesus before a friendly audience as was my own heart's desire. I went a number of times to such "all-religions-fellow-feeling" meetings, prepared my speeches, talked, prayed, listened, sang, smiled..., till I realized with unavoidable evidence what was obvious from the beginning, namely that those meetings were only a bland and elaborate waste of time.

Curiously, It was the reading of the works of another great disciple and helper of Gandhiji's that opened my eyes. Kishorlal Ghanshyamlal Mashruwala was Gandhiji's right-hand man in the field of philosophical principles and ethical values of his movement, as Kalelkar was in the field of education, Nehru in politics and Vinoba Bhave in social action. That great thinker, already dead, objected strongly and radically to such types of meetings, and he opposed Gandhiji himself who favoured them as a means to foster national unity and political peace. With wit and irony he called them "mixed-religion porridge", and his gastronomical sense of humour sharpened the edge of his ideological condemnation. A good dish of porridge can make a substantial breakfast, and I have swallowed many such breakfasts when in my early days in India I was submitted, with my companions, to a British diet which was meant, I guess, to set us in tune with history, though a little belatedly. But a mixture of all grains together tastes of none and spoils the breakfast. It was precisely a great Muslim emperor in India, Akbar, who invited to his court representatives of Islam, Hinduism and Christianity to make them resolve their differences and create a common religion, the Din-ilahi, to facilitate the union of the whole country and the government of its peoples. The hall he ordered expressly built for such meetings is still standing in his superb palace, and I was curious enough to visit it during a trip I made to North India. The hall is tall and square, with four running balconies half way up the four walls, to keep the teams separate and facing

111

one another. In one of the balconies sat the emperor with his ministers, in another the Islamic doctors, in the third one the Hindus, and in the fourth one the Christian priests who had come all the way from the West... with Francis Xavier's Jesuit nephew among them. I yielded to the impulse in me, which was more a tourist's whim than an act of devotion, to sit on the same approximate place my brother in religion must have occupied, knowing full well that his mission had ended in complete failure. The imperial porridge did not work.

The danger of such meetings is eclecticism, syncretism, minimalism, irenism, reduction to a common denominator, bland smiles, I pat your back and you pat mine, how nice you are! how nice we are! how nice we all are! let us all hold hands and dance together ring-a-ring-a-roses, losing our individual voices in the common chorus. The way to learn from other religions is not to mix them all, but, on the contrary, to let each one be itself with all its own originality and personality. There is no question of softening edges, but of respecting shapes; not of blurring colours but of discovering styles. Works of art are never to be tampered with. A classical picture is always a classical picture.

In Islam's picture I admire and want to learn the sense of dependence, of reverence, of humble worship before God's presence and will in all things. I have said that cheaply ecumenical meetings are usually a waste of time, but occasionally something can be learnt in them too. In one such meeting the Muslim speaker used a sentence that has remained fresh in my memory and forms part of my life ever since: "All that happens is God."

Every time I say the name of my own city, I recognize

112

the Islamic heritage within which I live: Ahmedabad. If I
pronounce "Ahmed" with a separated and aspirated "h",
"A-h-med", I proclaim the name of sultan Ahmed Shah
who founded it in the first half of the fifteenth century. I live
in a city founded by Islam, and I say it with pride.

SUGAR-AND-SALT DIALOGUE

"There are two kinds of Parsis", says one of them at the beginning of an article about his own community, that precious jewel and charming relic preserved in India, "those who work in the State Bank of India, and those who do not work in the State Bank of India." Parsi humour, typical and well-known, is a joyful consequence of their spiritual doctrine, and guarantees that one will always have a good time in their company, as has happened to me so many times. Another Parsi entitled a book he had written about his own religion "The Religion of the Good Life", with the double meaning of "leading a good moral life" and "having a good time in life": both are included in the teachings of their religion. Another Parsi, Zubin Mehta, born in Bombay, is conductor of New York's philarmonic orchestra as well as of the orchestra of the state of Israel; and still another Parsi, Jamshedji Tata, the founder of modern industry in India, has a whole city, Jamshedpur, dedicated to his name. All these seemingly disconnected points are explained by their religion, which is as interesting as it is unknown.

The Parsis are Persians, and the very similarity of the

115

two words is clear linguistic testimony to their racial and geographical origin. Their founder was Zoroaster or Zarathustra, a name which, in Western ears awakens the memory of "Thus spoke Zarathustra", though for some that will be a book by Nietzsche, and for others a symphonic poem by Strauss, and in any case will not tell readers or listeners much about the original doctrine of Zoroastrianism. His country was invaded by the Arabs centuries ago and Islam was made its official religion, so that a few Persians who wanted to keep their own faith embarked on ships, sailed away over the sea and eventually arrived at a shore that turned out to be India, near Surat in the present state (which is my state) of Gujarat. The story is told that when the unexpected guests asked the ruler of Surat permission to settle in his domains, he, in a symbolic gesture, sent to them a glass filled with milk up to the brim, meaning that there was no room for more people in his territory (apparently India has always been overpopulated; some consolation!); upon which the leader of the Parsis, not to be outdone in gesture and courtesy, added a few grains of sugar to the milk and returned the glass without spilling a drop. The ruler understood. The Parsis would mix with his people as the sugar in the milk. He gave his acquiescence. The Parsis disembarked. And the initial gesture of so many centuries ago has become actual history down to the present: the Parsis have lived among Hindus, Mohammedans and Christians as the sugar in the milk; kind, well-mannered, noble, zealous of their own identity and respectful of that of others. They are the only religious community that has never given any trouble in India. That is a fact of history, and we all have something to learn from it. Metaphors speak. We Christians are "the salt of the earth", while the Parsis are "the sugar in the milk". Salt seasons, heals, preserves, but it also itches and stings, and we Christians have caused some good itches

116

in history... in India and outside India. Language always implies theology, and, while we appreciate our own positions, we do well to want to know those of others. It is time for a dialogue between the sugar and the salt.

Parsi theology starts from the fundamental problem of the existence of both good and evil in the world, and to explain it, it postulates two original principles, one that creates and one that destroys; dangerous dualism that has raised eyebrows in scholastic circles, but which in fact is only a realistic reflection, however naive, of the play of light and shadow that is human life. The important conclusion is that as God is the Creator who defends his creation against the attacks of evil; man, by siding with creation, sides with God, that is, by siding with nature, by appreciating it and making use of it, by enjoying its good things and making them yield fruit, by indulging in action and activity, by giving himself up to work and to life... gives himself up to God; and so material progress becomes divine cult, and to have a good time is a duty and a virtue. This is to me the clearest case in the history of religions of the way the concept of God affects man's life, and how a theological principle creates an attitude and fosters a behaviour, thus shaping in a very concrete way the life and conduct of its followers. Once it has been established that working for nature is working for God, it follows that study, science, industry, research, art, the harnessing of natural resources, the refinement of life and even the enjoying of good food become practical commandments in the Zoroastrian decalogue, and having a good time is the best way of giving glory to God. That is why modern Indian industry has been created by the Parsis (though they are only a little over a hundred thousand in a country of six hundred millions), that is why their company always brings joy, and that is why some of my best meals have been as a

117

guest in Parsi homes. Theology becomes gastronomy, and dogma reaches the kitchen. If anyone believes that religion is not a practical thing, let him get himself invited by a Parsi family.

For a Parsi to fast is a sin, penance is an aberration, and celibacy a crime. Asceticism is simply immoral. Creation is meant to be perfected and enjoyed, not to be rejected. Matter is good, even food and sex, and to reject God's gifts is rejecting God. Worship has to be found in the midst of life, and liturgy is partaking of the banquet of creation. Moderation will always be there, of course, and nothing could be further from this attitude than any kind of licentiousness; but moderation must not be allowed to smother the enjoyment. To have a good time in this life is the best preparation to have a good time in the next. If you want to obtain eternal life, make the best of your temporal life.

I indulge here in a brief historical aside, which interests me particularly as a Christian. I have just now mentioned eternal life, the moral axis of the Christian vision. It is well-known that the old Hebrews did not have the concept of the immortality of the soul and the resurrection of the body as we have it. And it is not so well-known, though not less certain, that this concept entered into the Hebrew people during their Babylonian exile, that is, through the contact which at that time and place the children of Abraham had with the followers of Zoroaster. Jews, Christians and Mohammedans are in debt to the Parsis for this fundamental concept in their creed, or, putting it differently, God in his providence used Zoroaster and the Babylonian captivity to instill in his chosen people the essential doctrine of immortality and resurrection, which was to reach its climax in Jesus' own resurrection. The reviled Babylon turns out to have contributed something fundamental to the life of the heavenly

118

Jerusalem. In ecumenical terms (which have of late replaced the apocalyptic ones as literary genre) we could say that here we have the basis for a dialogue between the Beast and the Lamb.

What we Christians have not yet learned from the Parsis is the positive meaning of life, of matter, of pleasure. The old but persistent heritage of Manicheism and Gnosticism for which matter was evil, creation inimical, and pleasure sinful, weighs even now heavily on Christian morals. We are still smarting from the wound. We still feel guilty when we have a good time, and have not learned to enjoy pleasure. If the resurrection of the flesh has any meaning it is that our body also has been created for joy and glory, and it is up to us to train it gently in this life that it may be ready for its own happiness in the next. Sexual morals, in which the body plays a prominent role and where we have been hardest and most ascetic, have been traditionally negative among us, and only recently have we woken up and are trying hastily to adapt our doctrinal rigidity to the healthy realism we seek between trial and error. The traditional Christian doctrine on marriage has always been in its essence the one elaborated by a genius (St. Augustine) whose only experience of sex was fornication. It still hurts us there. Sex in itself is not over-important, but it can be an index and symbol of a general attitude to life and pleasure. There are still preachers in Christianity (and even more in Hinduism) who reduce all morals in practice to a single precept: Have a bad time in this life, in order to have a good time in the next. "To suffer or to die", "to suffer and not to die", "more sufferings, Lord, more!" are recorded exclamations of some of our best saints, and I understand and respect the mystical love from which they sprang, while at the same time I reject the abuses they have given rise to in

119

practice, and of which I myself have been a victim through many years. Just as orthodoxy can become sadistic (tortures inflicted on heretics), so asceticism can become masochistic (tortures inflicted on oneself), and both are dangerous deviations. Let us continue to be the salt of the earth, let us give the world taste and health, and even an occasional itch if necessary. But let us keep in mind that on a good table there must also be a sugar bowl.

The Parsis are known as "fire worshippers", which is not quite exact, as there is not precisely question of "worshipping", and in any case not of "fire" alone. It is not fire alone that the Parsis venerate, but the four elements, earth, air, fire and water, which essentially integrate and represent nature; and they are not worshipped as such, in fourfold physical idolatry as it were, but are rather seen as representing nature, and manifesting in it the presence and majesty of the Creator of all good things, before whom they bow in the direct vision of his creatures. A devout Parsi stands by the sea on Bombay's beautiful promenade whose geometry and glow have won for it the name of "The Queen's Necklace", bows with folded hands before the setting sun on the blue horizon of the Arabian sea, and feels the breeze that sends the day on its way beyond the elegant curve that Malabar Hill designs on the darkening waters. He is then performing a cosmic liturgy that recognizes the presence of the Creator in the world he has created, and says, as God said in Genesis and the Parsi reflects in his life, that the world is, and continues to be, good, indeed very good.

This closeness to nature, and to God in it, is the cause of the Parsis' material progress, but it also causes them a little problem at the hour of death, or rather, after death: what to do with the dead body? It cannot be buried, since enclosing the uncleanness of a decomposing body in the inside of

120

mother earth would be disrespectful to it, and thereby to nature, and thereby to God; for the same reason it would be sacrilege to throw it into the fire or the water, or to leave it to decay in the open where the stench would soil the air. The solution to this posthumous riddle is the "Towers of Silence". No one has seen them from the inside, since respect for death forbids the sight, and when a plane flew over one of them to take photographs, the protest, not only of the Parsis but of the whole of Bombay, was unanimous and the execration condemned; but all know what they are. There, on the top of an open spiral inside the circular structure, is where the dead body is placed. The vultures know the rendezvous, and they know their task. Within minutes the corpse is cleaned to the bones, which are then calcined by the heat of India's sun and drained, pure mineral lime, by its rains. To some the ritual appears macabre, but, when one thinks of it, it is a clean solution, both logical and ecological, to man's last problem on earth: how to disappear doing good and causing no trouble. The only business that does not thrive among Parsis is that of funeral parlours.

Dealing here with Zoroastrianism I have spoken more of its rules of conduct than of its concept of God. But I have set down at the beginning of the book that concept and behaviour are two sides of the same coin, and that the way we behave is a translation into action of the image of God we have in our minds. The apparent "dualism" of the Parsis which attributes all that is good to the Creative Principle and therefore welcomes nature and life in all their fullness, is what comes through in the deep and charming existential optimism that rules their lives. Dualism is not kindly regarded in the West, and it would seem that we severe monotheists could have nothing to do with it; and yet when I hear a dear old lady I knew well, repeat in her elementary Catholic

121

theology, "All good things come from God, and all bad things from the Devil", I fancy that Zoroaster has disciples among good Christians as well without their realizing it. Could we say... "anonymous Parsis" perhaps? Let us learn, at least, to enjoy the good things, as all come from God.

THOU SHALT ADORE THE
LORD YOUR NON-GOD

To me that is the most interesting religious situation in the world: a religion without God. Jainism has temples, images, liturgy, it has the purest morals I know (both in theory and in practice), it has holy scriptures and monks and nuns of exemplary observance, it has a church and an ecclesiastical hierarchy...; the only thing it lacks is God. It is an atheistic religion, an anonymous creed, a throne, most beautiful and ornate, but empty. It proclaimed two thousand five hundred years before Bonhoeffer his "religion without God" (which for him was also, logically, Christianity without Christ). The Jains form the most consistent and logical religious group I know, and it is from them that I have learned most in my own religious adventure. They reciprocate my affection and call me an "honorary Jain", a compliment which I gratefully accept. If the length of this chapter turns out to be proportionate to my own interest in Jainism, I foresee it is going to be a long chapter.

I go straight to the point, and let the folklore come afterwards. Why are the Jains atheists while they are deeply and unequivocally religious? For the very reason which is the main theme and inspiration of this book: the ultimate and transcendental respect of God as Supreme Being above all we can express or conceive. They know that they cannot worthily conceive the idea of God, and consequently they keep quiet about him. That is all. It is the veil of the tabernacle, but placed already before the mind itself that it may not even think of God. The Jains are the most logical people in my experience, and the most exaggerated in carrying their philosophical principles to their last practical consequences. They know it and accept their own exaggerations of which I soon will give examples. They abhor compromise, and maybe that is why I get on so well with them. Now, those exaggerated attitudes act for me as a magnifying glass which allows me to see, as in a laboratory, the detail and the secret of motives and attitudes in my own life with their consequences. Such an analysis is immensely valuable. And it is that same exaggeration that leads them to live without God whom they secretly adore without realizing it themselves. It is worth examining this point in some detail with the magnifying glass they generously lend us.

I come back to the basic commandment. "You shall not make images of God." The Mohammedans keep it faithfully, and never express God's image in paintings or sculptures. The Hebrews obey it too even more rigorously, as they do not even pronounce the name of God. That is, they do not permit even a verbal image, let alone a pictorial or sculptural image. The name Yahweh in the Bible is not a name as such, but only a code, a password, a linguistic trick to make reference to God without pronouncing his name; it is a word puzzle of four consonants, Y-H-W-H, unpronounceable in themselves, with their gaps to be filled at will as Yehowah (Jehovah), Yahweh or other vowels, so as to know whom

124

we are mentioning without mentioning him. And now the Jains go one step further in the observance of this fundamental commandment, they go beyond Mohammedans and Hebrews, and reach the ultimate logic as is their wont. If our brushes taint God's image when painting it, and our lips sully his name when pronouncing it, even more will our thoughts debase his concept when conceiving it. Let us then observe silence, not only with our brushes and our lips, but with our thought; and rather than think of God anything unworthy of him (as will necessarily be the case when the thinking instrument is the human brain, narrow and limited), let us stop thinking of him altogether. Thus the Jain's silence is his profession of faith, his atheism is worship, his denial is devoted assertion.

The Jain does not say all this to himself in so many words, in fact he does not say it at all. He does not argue out, "In order not to debase the concept of God, whom I adore, I am not going to think of him, though all the time I know very well he exists"; he does not say that, he does it, that is, he simply does not think of him, does not refer to him, does without him, lives without him, is a neat and perfect atheist from birth to death; his holy scriptures explain the world without a Creator, and his elaborate morals work without a Supreme Being. The Jain makes himself a radical atheist in order to save his Father's honour. Supreme sacrifice.

I now come down (or go up) to the philosophical level, and whoever wants to have nothing to do with metaphysics can freely skip this paragraph. There is question here of the "analogy of being", Aristotelian cornerstone of Western thought and Christian theodicy. I can call God "Father" (I have done so in the last paragraph with nobody objecting), because the word "father" can, while keeping a basic common meaning, be applied in a very different way to a man who is a father in a human family, and to God who is our Father in heaven. That is, in essence, the "analogy" of two concepts, human father and Heavenly Father, together similar and different, expressed in one single word, father (and may my metaphysics professor, who is still around, forgive me for such a clumsy explanation). Now then, Jainism does not recognize the analogy of being. In it there are no "analogous" concepts, but purely "univocal" ones, which apply in exactly the same way to each case. That destroys the conceptual bridge between man and God. How can I say now that God is Father, when the word and concept "father" are used for something so limited and imperfect as is a man who is a father here on earth? How can I say that God "exists", when the only existing we know is this painful and flimsy living of our own experience? How can I say that God "loves", when the verb "to love" has such unacceptable meanings down here? I can say nothing of God, I can think nothing of God. Earth is cut off from heaven. Without a fitting philosophy there is no theology. The analogy of being, abstract and academic thesis of my student days, acquires an unexpected importance in practical consequences. In the long run it is ideas that count.

All this does not prevent the Jains from coming with fervour to their temples, marble filigree in Dilwara, labyrinth of a thousand columns in Ranakpur, sacred mountain where each stone is a shrine in Palitana. Their prayer is an examination of conscience, their sacraments are personal purification, and the objects of their "cult" are the twenty-four prophets of Jainism. These have certainly their images, or rather, image, as all are identical, their sculptural monotony being a logical result of their philosophical "univocity". A religion, however atheistic it may be, needs a

126

cult and a liturgy and a ritual, and Jainism is no exception. On the contrary, it rather fills up the empty space of its non-dogma with the richness of its devotions. The ("divine"?) cult in the Jain temples is the most methodical, complex and regular in the whole of India. The exquisite neatness of their aisles and naves is image and reflection of the purity of their morals.

I have been invited to the ceremony of the "religious profession" of a young monk. I know the family and the boy who has taken a brilliant degree in economics and has a bright future ahead in his studies and in his father's business, but who has left everything to embrace for life the proverbial austerity of the Jain monks. On the eve of the ceremony he threw a party "to bid farewell to the world", and I attended that too, and heard him say, before relatives and friends, some words that made me think. He said: "I want from you all this prayer and this blessing, that if at the end of this life I do not obtain the final liberation and have to be born again", (according to the universal belief in reincarnation and the transmigration of souls)..., "I may be born into a Jain family." I was touched by his faith.

Thousands of people have gathered for the ceremony. The candidate arrives in solemn procession, dressed in costly vestments and loaded with jewels, and the cavalcade is called "the nuptial procession", since religious profession, in their culture as well as in ours, is called and considered a ritual of nuptials. (Nuptials... with whom? Do we not sense there the presence of the Ever Absent though never mentioned?). On arrival he takes off all his ornaments, of double value now as jewels and as relics, and they are auctioned there and then among the devout public at enhanced prices. The Jains are the richest community in India (their own honesty having contributed to their prosperity), and they

127

generously finance their temples, cult, religious functions, restoration, and institute scholarships and provide help of all kinds for those of their community, and others too, who are in need. There are no poor people among the Jains. Another paradox of the religion that preaches and practices the greatest detachment in the world... and in which nobody lacks anything. Let us go on with the ceremony.

The candidate is now dressed in white. I know that the young monk belongs to the sect of the *swetambars* ("white-vestment"), and I call to mind with sorrow that the Jains have not been spared the curse of divisions within a religion. The rival sect is that of the *digambars* ("direction-vestment") whose monks go about dressed in "the four directions of the wind", that is, stark naked. Radical commitment, total detachment, Jain thouroughness, live image of naked poverty which, in its virginal Adamitic innocence, reminds, with its awkward presence, a sophisticated and suspicious world of the original simplicity and the final destiny of the human race. Pure Jainism, always ready with logic and surprise.

Now comes the tonsure. We had something similar done to us, candidates to the Catholic priesthood, when, as an introduction to the "minor orders", the bishop's scissors cut a tuft of our hair, so that from then on we sported a crew cut, with the crown of the head shaved to proclaim to the world our consecration by our very presence. The Jain tonsure is as all Jain things, more radical. The young man dressed in white is now standing in the middle of the central platform in the open air where the ceremony is taking place, and four older monks approach him. The four stand around him, and begin to pluck out with their bare fingers small tufts of hair from his head, and to lay them reverently on an open handkerchief in the hands of the candidate's father who

128

stands by to receive them. From time to time they stop, and rub the boy's head with a mixture of sandalwood powder and ashes which heals and disinfects. The young man smiles stoically, and I, when I look at him, feel a shiver of sacred tenderness run through my sinful body. From today onwards the consecrated man will repeat the operation every six months, only that he will do it himself with his own hands; ascetical self-depilation, bodily renovation of vows, consecration of the head, and in it of the mind and the thought, to the total commitment. The bishop's scissors were certainly easier.

The Jain religious takes five vows which he or she observes faithfully for life. Always to tell (and live) the truth, not to cause harm to anybody or anything, not to possess anything, not to desire to possess anything, and to keep perfect chastity. From then on the young monk will live daily on alms. Every morning he will knock at the door of a Jain house (to ensure the legal purity of the food), and will eat standing, out of his open hands, whatever they give him..., and so till the following day. He will sleep doubled up on the floor, his knees touching his chin, in order to "possess" as small a portion of the earth as possible. He will not use a lamp at night, so as not to attract and destroy insects in its flame. He will suffer the winter cold and the summer heat in a single garb. And he will confess openly before all any negligence he may have incurred in the observance of the rules.

An essential ceremony still remains. The change of name. The consecrating guru will utter it in his ear at the auspicious moment determined by the friendly stars and minutely calculated by the astrology which presides over everything in India. The change in name is and signifies the change in life, in behaviour, in personality. The name will be

129

long and will carry embedded in it the word *vijay* which means "victory" and which linguistically comes from the same root as "Jain". A Jain is a man who has obtained victory over himself. The name is made public, and the respectful crowd shouts it together in unison. A monk is born.

And now the young monk starts on his way... and never stops for the rest of his life. That is, perhaps, the hardest observance of his vocation. He will never spend more than three days at a stretch in the same place. The old Christian monks used to make a vow of "stability", that is, of remaining in the same monastery for life; instead, the Jain monks add to their five fundamental vows the promise of "mobility", which means never to have "where to lay their heads", to spend their whole life walking, on their feet, on the road, changing their fleeting home from temple to temple in a pilgrimage without end. They do this for two reasons. One, to preach with their feet the essential sermon that life itself is a pilgrimage (towards God?); and another, to protect the vow of poverty. However careful the religious may be in observing poverty, possessions pile up. I have been living twentyfive years in the same Jesuit house, and if any day I have to move, I will need a truck. A fixed residence multiplies luggage. But the Jain monk has to carry bodily all his possessions, and that imposes a severe physical limitation on earthly attachments. There they go, walking barefoot in the first hours of the day before India's sun raises the fury of the asphalt on the road against their naked feet, a shy bundle on their shoulder, with a step made brisk by daily practice, precursors of jogging, prophets of distances, apostles of the road, professionals in contingency, always ahead, always on the way to another home, always on the move that the heart may never get struck. Heroic instability which ensures purity of life. Only during the rainy season

130

are they allowed to stay in one place, and that is for another more important consideration that takes preference over poverty. With the torrential rains, the air and the soil seethe with insects, as anybody who has experienced an Indian monsoon knows only too well, and to walk in such a milieu would cause harm to those minimal beings whom we are bound to protect with special care for their frailness. The vow of not harming any creature outrules the vow of poverty, and so, while the rains last, the monk does not move.

The main vow the monk takes, and the fundamental commandment Jainism upholds, is that of not causing any harm to anybody, the respect for life, non-violence. Here "life" (again the analogy of being) is a "univocal" concept, that is, life in man, in an animal, and even in the smallest plant, has exactly the same value and dignity; that is why the commandment "thou shalt not kill" covers also the humblest insect and the blade of grass. The Jain monk carries always with him a white broom, and uses it to sweep carefully any place in which he plans to rest, so that the tiniest of creatures may not inadvertently be crushed to death when he sits down. Respect for life in all its manifestations is the first and greatest of all Jain commandments. And here comes something even more curious: to the Jain even the air and the earth and the mountains and the rocks have a soul, are alive with the same life that pulsates in all beings, and which, if it does not appear in a stone, is only because the body of the stone does not have the organs the human body has, it does not have a tongue, for instance, and thus it cannot speak; but the life in it is essentially the same as in man, and has to be respected with the same dedication. Cosmic commandment whose reach is measured in light years. Ecological religion *par excellence*, which enjoins reverence for the whole of creation, since the whole of it is alive. And

131

here, too, the Jain tendency to exaggerate reaches difficult, if logical, extremes. A Jain cannot be a farmer, because to drive a plough through the earth would be stabbing in cold blood her living breast; cannot be a doctor (or rather, could not, since modern life is forcing its way through, and talented young Jains have challenged the precept and are excellent doctors) because, in his training, he would have to use his scalpel on animals, and that is sacrilege; he cannot travel by plane (here again, laymen do it now, but not so the monks), since the plane in flight rips brutally through the wind with the cutting edge of its wings, and grinds and tortures the air in the sadistic turbines of the modern jet. The first (and only) time when a Jain monk boarded a plane to travel abroad on a religious mission, a group of young Bombay Jains surrounded the plane to prevent its taking off. The Jain community venerates its monks to excess, but it also takes care that they keep their rules. The plane finally took off..., and the monk ceased to be a monk. This is, by the way, one of the reasons why Jainism is so little known outside India. Jainism does not travel.

The Jain monk wears always before his mouth a piece of cloth, immaculately white, that hangs from his ears and hides his face from the nose down. Tourists who notice the strange sight and ask for an explanation are usually told that the monks do that in order not to swallow inadvertently some insect (which would be entomological cannibalism). That is not the true explanation. The Jain monks are not so clumsy as to go on swallowing flies as they walk. The true explanation is more subtle. They wear a veil before the mouth in order not to hurt with their breath the air when they talk. The air is a living being, and our pronounciation (think of plosive "p") stabs its delicate texture and makes it suffer. The white veil before the mouth holds the breath and

132

stops the blow. Franciscan thoughtfulness with brother air. Though it proves to be rather irritating for the person who speaks with them, or at least it is so for me, and I tell them so plainly. Once I was giving a lecture to about a hundred Jain nuns, that is, to a hundred half faces and a hundred while veils neatly arranged in rows before me. Now, when I talk I like to see my listeners, and it helps me to watch the effect of my words as reflected on their faces; but here I had only the broken mirrors of the half faces to watch. I said: "I am determined to have a good time with you, and I'm not going to be satisfied until I get your smiles to show beyond your little white rags." They laughed so heartily that I realized how when a person really smiles it is not only her lips that smile, but her whole face, as the eyes, brows, foreheads and cheeks of those loveable Sisters burst into sincere joy in spontaneous person-to-person communication. I had a grand time with those splendid Sisters. None of them, however, unlocked the veil from even one ear, and the true ascetical tradition was upheld.

I am going to indulge here in a cultural jump to tell quite a different anecdote and sharpen contrasts. I was once in Spain addressing another group of Sisters, though these were Catholic and had no veil over their mouths; and I was talking to them precisely of those remote and unknown sisters of theirs, the Jain nuns of India, and of the exemplary pure and abnegated life they lead, though they do not believe in God. When I thought I had made things clear to them, a Sister asked me with sadness and surprise: "Father, those religious Sisters do not believe in God...; but at least they'll believe in Our Lady, isn't it?" Ecumenism has still a large gap to bridge between religion and religion.

All those vows, commandments and customs in Jainism spring from a deep common root: the law of *karma*.

133

The word itself has travelled, through Hinduism and occultism, to the languages of the West where it is used more or less fittingly with various meanings; but the origin and practice, again exaggerated, of the principle it entails, are to be found in Jainism. *Karma* in Sanskrit means "action", and the law of karma simply states that whatever one suffers or enjoys at a particular moment, has been determined by his previous actions in this life and in preceding ones according to the universal belief in reincarnation. The general idea is that "man reaps what he sows", only that the principle is not applied in a remote and general way, but in a fixed, concrete and metaphysically unavoidable way. The whole universe is an immense clockwork into which all actions of all beings are inscribed in full detail, so that the same machinery in due time places each one in the pleasant or painful circumstances determined by his previous conduct. All this is done without any intervention on the part of a just and merciful God who judges and forgives, hands over reward or punishment; but only through the inner balance of the universe itself which automatically fills up, so to speak, moral gaps with penal retribution.

After living many years in India one comes to feel the strength of the principle of karma, for ever present in every attitude and every circumstance, the hold it has on the mind of the people, and the consequent fact that the Orient cannot be understood without it. I want to try and explain and communicate this feeling, as far as is possible, to readers who may not be familiar with the idea, and who may want to know how one half of humankind reacts before the fundamental problems that affect us all. I take the case of a family, pious and healthy, in which a child has been born blind, and another child fully healthy and sound. How to explain that inequality? What does Christian piety say when it looks upon this newborn baby who will live, yes, and possibly a long life, but will never see sunlight and never contemplate his mother's face? It accepts God's supreme will and his inscrutable judgements in the free distribution of his gifts, and humbly follows his mysterious designs with the hope that both the child who has been born with sight and the one who has been born without it may be happy (there are sightless people who are happy, and sighted who are not), and both may come to see God, which is the true and eternal happiness. That is a deep and worthy attitude, full of faith and reverence for God's supreme dominion over his creatures. On the other hand it is good to realize that nobody in the world accepts such an attitude outside Christians, Jews and Mohammedans—and we form but a fraction of humanity. For any Indian it is simply unthinkable that God could, out of his own pure free will, create a child with eyes and another without them. That would be a radical injustice, an intolerably whim, a procedure totally unworthy of God. Inequality at birth is an undeniable reality, and it is even more striking in India given its large population and the sharp contrasts it gives rise to. Why is a child born poor and another rich? Why is one born strong and another weak? And why—supreme and agonizing question in the context of the castes which even today influence a man's future more than any other factor—why is a man born a Brahmin and another man an untouchable?

We cannot soil God's name with the stain of that whimsical decision. We cannot burden God with the responsibility of that initial election which favours one and crushes the other from his mother's womb. We must find a cause, a reason that will explain the difference and exonerate God from the creational caprice which marks one child for abundance and another for pain even before he is born. And that reason is the law of karma. The kind and circumstances of birth in this life are determined in full by the person's behaviour in his previous life. It is not God who decides that, but the person himself with his previous behaviour. This child is born blind because he made wrong use of his eyes in his previous life; he is born untouchable because he had been proud (I am quoting the Jain scriptures); he is born without hands because he was a thief, or dumb because he lied in court. We feel sorry for the child, but when he misbehaved he wrote his own sentence, and he knew it. He did what was evil in his past life, and has to pay for it in this one; that is all. This explains inequality at birth, and not only that but also all ensuing trials in life. Why should this happen to me? Why has this suffering suddenly overtaken me? Because I had unpaid bills in the account of my own conscience. Human behaviour has to be audited, and debts have to be settled. That is painful, yes, for me and for all, but at least it is clear and just, and safeguards God's holiness. Karma is the ultimate explanation of all that happens in life. That is why in India the word karma is on everybody's lips. My best professor of dogmatic theology in Poona used to say: "Karma is the law of the metaphysical congruence of the universe."

An image. I am with a Jain family struck by suffering. The smallest son, a charming child hardly five years old, has had an attack of polio and will remain a cripple for life. His mother tells me while the child himself listens: "My poor dear son! He is so good and so obedient! Yet he will never be able now to walk straight in his life. And the suffering affects me, his mother, as much as it affects him. In our past lives both he and I must have done something wrong; now we have to pay for it. It is bad enough, but still it is good to

136

pay all debts as soon as possible, particularly those of the soul. That will give us strength to bear this trial with resignation, and to console ourselves thinking that this suffering purifies us and makes us clean and free for the next life. And I will love my son more than ever and will look after him with all my soul. He is my dearest child now!" And she embraces him with motherly love. I see and live that whole scene in my own heart, and think to myself: What difference is there between Jain resignation and Christian resignation?

This visceral belief in karma is the motive and motor of the strict and rigorous morality Jains observe in practice. The Jain is convinced that the law will be fulfilled with mathematical inevitability (in this he differs from the Hindu for whom God, in his mercy, can obliterate man's karma), and that if he cheats in this life he will be a beggar in the next, if he commits adultery he will become a widower, if he harbours low desires he will be born mentally retarded; and in that conviction he finds strength and courage to stay away from adultery and fraud and any kind of ignoble behaviour. Once more history confirms theology, and morals answer dogma: in the matter of purity of life and honourable behaviour the Jain community stands first among all religious communities I know. I do admit that they are low in feelings and high in pride; but in sheer moral cleanliness of daily behaviour they are exemplary and have no rival. The law of karma works.

To get rid of the acquired karma the only way is to bear its consequences. This way, however, can be shortened in practice by adding voluntary penances to those that life brings us. This realization has converted the Jains into champions of penance and specialists in asceticism. Here I do not speak any more of monks and nuns, but of married men and women in their families. Fasting is the Jains' favourite hobby. They fast at the slightest provocation, and they have a variety of ways to do it which defies imagination. I describe only one way for the sake of brevity. One day of fast (eating nothing at all in twenty-four hours) followed by one day of half fast (only one frugal meal a day) followed by two days of fast and one of half fast, three of fast and one of half first..., and so on till eight continuous days of fast and one of half fast, and then backwards, seven days of fast and one half fast, six of fast and one half fast... down to one day of fast, and the necessary rest and restoring strength for the next programme. Number eight in that exercise is a minimum goal; it goes up from there, and I know cases of thirty. If anyone wants to calculate the number of days the whole exercise takes when the number is thirty, he will be astonished at the figure, and at the endurance of those confirmed penitents. Others fast for simply a number of days or weeks at a stretch without eating anything. And all those fasts are known and commented upon in the whole neighbourhood. Favourite topic for daily gossip among housewives: "Have you heard? She has reached forteen days without a bite!"—"That's nothing; her neighbour has sworn she'll reach a month this time."—"We shall see about that."—"If my husband had not fallen sick, you would have seen what I can do; but now I reserve myself for next year." Olympics of fasting, with records and prizes and medals. The family gives a party when one of its members successfully concludes a long fast, the emaciated hero or heroine is congratulated and garlanded, and his or her photo is published in the daily papers. I know all this, and, not without a touch of mischief, and an air of innocence I sometimes read out to them the Sermon on the Mount: "When you fast, wash your face and perfume your head, so that nobody may know you have fasted..."; and they look at one another and laugh. I have caught them redhanded.

138

This chapter is getting out of bounds, and I want to bring it to an end. I cannot, however, omit, for its close connection with the fundamental theme of this book, the parable that Jainism has given to the world, and which is now repeated in all literatures, without references to its forgotten origin. It is the parable of the blind men and the elephant. Some blind men, who did not know what an elephant was, were placed near one, so that they might touch it with their hands and then describe it each in his own way. One said: it is like a column; another: like a wall; another: like a ceiling; another: like a rope; another: like a fan; another: like a horn; another: like a hose. Each one expressed what he had felt with his hands: the leg, the side, the belly, the tail, the ear, the tusk, the trunk. We are, of course, the blind men, and the elephant is...? To complete the parable I add that another blind man just kept feeling the air and said nothing.

Finally comes death. The moment of truth. If death is witness and reflection of what life has been, death in India (and here I speak of both Hindus and Jains) bears witness to the peace of soul its religions proclaim and its followers attain. Death in India is easier than in Europe or America in the sense that here one dies with greater ease, greater serenity and naturalness, without giving the matter undue importance, without making a fuss or setting the bells tolling in bereavement. In the West each person has only one life, one death, one eternity, one heaven and one hell ahead in a unique and irreversible decision once and for ever; and that weighs heavily at the moment of taking the plunge. In India the soul has practised many times the change over, and it takes leave with the easy gesture of the brief encounter... till we meet again! Belief in the transmigration of souls makes death easier and softens its blow. There is always the pain of parting, and a certain mist of uncertainty which never quite clears up; but there is no grip of fear of a last judgement, no trauma of final responsibility in the once-for-all test. The wheel of karma keeps going round and round, and there are still many turns to go. The rhythm of birth and death is nature's own rhythm, and the soul has learned to swing with it. In life's ongoing examination, death for an Indian is an easy subject. Tagore expressed the idea in genial poetry: "The child is sucking at his mother's breast when... the milk gets over! The child cries, thinking that his joy is over for ever. His mother notices it at once, and gently changes the child to the other breast which is full. That is death. Passing from one breast of mother nature to the other... with a brief tear in between." Only a short time ago I followed with love the death of the father of my best Jain friend, and that was the way he died.

Mahatma Gandhi was not a Jain, he was a Hindu, but his ayah was a Jain, and the only person whose advice in religious matters Gandhi sought when his Christian friends in South Africa urged him to consider the Christian option and he did so with his unflinching sincerity was a Jain saint, Kavi Rajchandra, whose written answers on this subject to Gandhiji are still extant (and I feel a great urge to quote them now, but they do not fit here). Gandhiji hailed from Gujarat, and in this state (which is mine) Jain influence is particularly felt because, due to historical reasons, most of the Jains in India live here, and, though in numbers they are a very small minority, their presence is felt in their faith, their prestige and their zeal. It was through these channels that Gandhiji learned from Jainism the doctrine of non-violence; with it he obtained India's independence through peaceful means. The greatest historic deed of our times, a great country becoming independent without a war of independence, drew its basic inspiration from Jainism. This original conviction was strengthened, on Gandhiji's own testimony, by his reading of the Sermon on the Mount ("... offer the other cheek"), as also by the teachings of Hinduism and the example of the mythological saint Prahlad who suffered indignities without offering any resistance. Thus he united several beliefs in the great creed that inspired his life, strengthened his hand and gave him victory. And its first root he found in Jainism.

I come back, at the end of the chapter, to my first fundamental idea. The behaviour of a religious group reflects their concept of God, and consequently among the Jains the extreme purity of the non-concept has created the rigid rule of duty for duty's sake, the non-transferable responsibility each one has for his own karma, the imperative of a logic without mitigation, and the ultimate serenity before death. Atheistic morality that supplies dry strength in the loneliness of one's personal effort. We can learn from the Jain experience how to understand atheism, how to correct our excessively anthropomorphic concept of God, how to save from the fires of the Inquisition apparent atheists whose silence is only reverence for the mystery, and how not to abuse and misuse God's mercy to justify and make possible and easy the moral false steps of our own behaviour.

I am aware that I have been partial to Jainism. While shortening this already long chapter I have omitted negative aspects, and I know it. Let the positive picture remain so as to provide a better contrast and elicit a sharper reaction. This can be for the good of all. After all I am an honorary Jain (only honorary; I shudder at their penances)..., and a confirmed Catholic.

141

THE POWER OF THE MONSOON

The rainy season, or the monsoon, is called in India the "four-month", as indeed it lasts four months, July to October in my region, and separates the dry and hot summer from the dry and temperate winter. This does not imply that for all four months it rains all the time, day and night, but that the entire rainfall of the year is confined to those four months; and some times, yes, it rains with such intensity and violence, it seems as though the clouds make up for the eight months in which they are forbidden to release a single drop of water, whatever the need of the parched earth or of the parched people on the land. The rain comes down in waterfalls, without warning, converts streets into rivers in a matter of minutes, and mocks umbrellas and raincoats putting them out of use in the wet whirlwind that fills everything, gets into everything, floods and soaks everything leaving no defence except resignation and patience and the changing one's clothes when one reaches home... which at least will be dry if one has been wise enough to close and lock all windows before leaving.

The power to put up with inconveniences is a national

143

virtue in India, and people know how to get wet with good grace, with style and elegance; they know how to smile under the rain, how to walk with their clothes sticking to the body and their hair dripping wet, themselves almost part and parcel of the drenched landscape, of the humid event that revitalizes the whole earth during the four months. In that I have not yet become an Indian, and I still feel annoyed when I get wet, I resent being caught in the rain, and I worry under the Western superstition that if I get wet I will catch a cold. For that reason I go out as little as possible during the monsoon, as the Jain monks do, though for different reasons as I have explained. Still, during the many years in which I lived begging my way from house to house (in that I did behave like a Jain monk), I had of necessity to come daily at eleven in the morning to take my classes in college. and go back at five in the afternoon to whatever house I was lodging at for the day. I always came and went on a bicycle; that meant pedalling my way for half an hour through the anarchy of peak hour traffic, through impossible streets and traffic lights that stand there just for the show of it. I enjoy cycling in itself, the cycle being one of the most efficient machines ever invented by man in effort-output relationship, without problems of parking or dependence on petrol, and with a continuous view of the street on all sides and all the people on it, so that a hand raised in time is enough to greet a friend in the homely city. But during the "four-month" my beloved cycle became an instrument of torture. The rain. If anyone has not experienced what it is to pedal in the rain, let him try it. The dark curtain of water, the flooded street that hides under the current the treacherous potholes, the helpless waiting in the traffic jams under the unremitting deluge, the flood at half-wheel height giving me the impression I am practising water-skiing rather than going to conduct a mathematics class. I dreaded the sky on those days,

144

and when the hour of taking my bicycle approached I would look anxiously through the window and question the clouds. Will it rain? Will it hold?

Then I would turn to God in prayer. Lord, don't let it rain! Hold back the clouds for this half hour that it takes me to reach the college. You have the whole day and night to send down your rain, you rule the climate and regulate the seasons. You are Lord of heaven and earth, the clouds obey your word, and not a drop of water comes down from the heavens without your permission. You see me and love me and care for me with greater dedication, as you yourself said, than a mother for her own son. If it were for my mother to decide now whether it is going to rain or not, you know very well that it would not rain. And, are you going to do less? I believe in your promises, in your word, in your commitment when you said "ask and you shall receive", and with that absolute trust in you I now ask you to restrain your showers for this half hour and let me reach my destination dry. I thank you for having heard my prayer, and go joyfully into the street trusting in your love and your power. Amen.

Those were the days of my great charismatic fervour, and I positively enjoyed having this occasion to commit my whole being to prayer, particularly to this concrete and courageous petitionary prayer which is the measure of one's faith and commitment to God. To pray for the salvation of souls and the welfare of humanity is all very well, but, since the results cannot be measured, it is a soft and comfortable prayer which does not commit the one who makes it and leaves no imprint on the soul. But asking with direct hope that it may not rain on my way the next half hour, is coming out into the open, risking one's faith and facing the consequences which will be known very soon. For me that

145

committed prayer was such a joy that I welcomed this daily opportunity to practise it, and I put myself into it with all my heart. Even if it was raining cats and dogs in the morning, I dared to ask that the deluge would stop when the time came for me to move. If God's power has no limit, why should my faith in him have any? And I would again temper my faith in the fire of petition. The rainy season thus became for me a season of fervour and grace.

More than once I have left the house under a threateningly black sky, run my way on the brink of a watery disaster, just reached the safety of the college porch, and at that very moment, when I was already under cover, the gates of heaven opened and the whole world was filled with water. At such times I smiled contented in the firmness of my faith. Thank you, Lord! You have held back the clouds with your own hand, as it were, watching carefully for the moment I was safe, and withdrawing at that very instant your protecting fingers to let the monsoon have its way. What a joy it is to see your power and to feel your love in the tangible reality of your daily protection in my minimal needs! Not a hair of our heads falls without your ordering it, and not a drop of water leaves the clouds without your permission. Truly you are Father and you are Lord, and it is a joy to live in your house and under you care. If you take care that I should not get wet today, how much more will you take care that my soul may not come to harm and I may remain safe in body and soul now and for eternity! Blessed be the rain that waters my faith into flower!

Such was not always the case, though. At times I was caught squarely in the rain and was drenched through and through before I could reach the now useless college porch. On those occasions I used to redouble my petitionary efforts, and I thought and said: I have got wet, Lord, in spite

146

of my prayer and my faith; but I accept the drenching at your hands, I respect your judgements and I admit that, even though I do not understand your way of acting, it does answer, in the mystery of your providence, my ardent prayers; and whatever you do for me you do for my good, and so I offer you again my thanks, wet this time, but as fervent and sincere as when I arrive dry. And tomorrow I will pray again in the face of the clouds as though nothing had happened today. Blessed be your name for ever.

Those were my experiences and my reflections all through the four months. Everything was running smoothly; dry or wet, I would always find a way to justify God and strengthen my faith. Yet is was also a fact that the repeated incidence of the prayer-cum-drenching experience was beginning to cause some tension in my mind, a tension that went on secretly increasing as the showers inevitably hit their target again and again, since four months are many days, and the monsoon winds are wet winds. It is easy to react favourably the first time and to come out from the disappointment with flying colours; but in the long run honestly little by little imposes itself, and the forced thanksgiving with dripping clothes and shivering bones becomes more and more difficult. The tension, which I was hiding from myself and did not want to recognize, was dangerously increasing under the monsoon clouds.

One day I was about to reach in safety with the song of praise on my lips when at the very last moment the clouds burst, the rain poured down and I was helplessly caught in it just before I reached the harbour. I could not resist the complaint. Lord, couldn't you have waited for one minute? And the next day the same story. That was too much. I could not go on dissembling before God and before myself. I could sense how the hidden resentment and frustration at the futility of my efforts to reconcile my prayers with the undeniable facts were growing within me. Finally one day, after a similar experience, I dried and cleaned my cycle as best I could, went to the chapel still dripping wet, and told the Lord with great peace and serenity: "My relationship with you is more important to me than getting or not getting wet in the rain, and I see that my petitionary efforts are jeopardizing that relationship instead of strengthening it as I had hoped. I cannot fight against reality and tell you that I am delighted and thank you heartily when I have asked you to let me arrive without getting wet, and I arrive like a bedraggled hen. You know me well, and you know that I do not like to be formal or artificial and say what I do not feel. Let us have done with this, and it will be better for both. From this moment on and for ever I free you from any obligation you may have to hear my prayers on account of your promises, however clear and repeated they may be in your own Gospel, so that you remain at liberty to deal with me as you think best in any circumstance. Let the monsoon work as though I did not exist, and do not worry about having to change meteorological conditions for my sake. And the same holds good for any other happening in my life. I want you to act with full freedom and without any kind of restriction, and do not feel bound to live up to my expectations of you or fulfill the hopes I have about you. Only one thing, I also understand that by the same account I too remain free to behave before you as I think best in each case, even if my behaviour does not respond to your official requirements. And let our relationship be closer than ever."

It was such a natural and spontaneous gesture that I myself was taken by surprise. But the peace it brought me from the first moment and the increase in intimacy with God that it subsequently brought told me clearly that the gesture

148

had been deep and genuine. It was to have a great influence in my life, and that is why I have described it in detail. The first effect it had was to reconcile me with the monsoon. Till then I had feared the rain and hated getting drenched. Now I began to mind it less. And I understood why. The rain formerly brought me two evils: the drenching, and, far worse, the resentment against God who had promised to hear me and had not done so, resentment which was all the more dangerous and harmful as I did not want to recognize it and covered it up with forced alleluias. Now I continued to get wet just as before, since the clouds followed their course as they had always done, but there was only one evil for me: the drenching. There was no resentment any more, and the very absence of resentment made the drenching more bearable; there was only question now of drying myself and changing my clothes, without the former mystical acrobatics to justify my getting wet in spite of my prayers. Now I got wet just as everybody gets wet when caught under a downpour, and that was all. There was no monsoon tragedy for me any more, only letting nature follow its course and accepting it with equanimity. Four months of peace.

I say that it was a spontaneous and unexpected gesture, and that is true, but when analysing it quietly in the following days, I understood that it had been preceded by a long preparation. First, the close range preparation of the rainy days with their tide of conflicting feelings rising within me under pressure from the clouds, then the attitude of clarity and sincerity before God which already ruled my relationship with him, and, at long range, the fertile contact with other religions and their ways of understanding God and dealing with him, as I have described them in previous chapters which are only a preparation and explanation of this one. God was not limited by the concept I had had of

149

him till then (however beautiful and true and consoling and helpful it had truly been), and I was now ready to let him come out of the frame I had built for him and to let him face me in freedom. It took me much sincerity and many drenchings, but the resulting gain was transcendental. Whatever we gain in depth and truth and freedom in dealing with God, is gain in the meaning and reality of life through self-realization and God's greater glory, which can converge together if we understand them properly. Never had I an experience such as this.

Let me get things clear: it is not that I was freeing God from his promises, but that I had freed myself from the image of a God limited by his promises. That was the advance. I was holding on to an image which had accompanied me and sustained me for half a lifetime, and to allow now that image to yield and give way to a different and wider one, was for me a spiritual conquest. This was all the more consoling as the advance was in the direction of a greater freedom, and therefore a greater sovereignty, of God, and of a greater trust, and therefore greater intimacy, of me with him. To let God be God, to let him come out of his own rules and out of his own Gospel if he so desires. To let him be totally free, not in himself, which he is already from eternity, but in his dealings with me which were ruled, tied down, conditioned by traditions and promises and commandments and the ways I understood them which limited my vision of God and consequently my way of behaving towards him. All those rules and ordinations are legitimate and worthy of all respect, but God is above all that, and to recognize that is to worship him. That is the difficult liberation.

When I recognize in practice God's supreme freedom towards me, I receive in answer the free gift of a greater

150

freedom in myself towards him. I come back to the theme of this book, namely that the concept I have of God shapes my life and rules my conduct (at the same time that it reflects it and is fruit and result of it), and so when I conceive a freer God in his dealings with me, I in turn acquire a greater freedom in my dealings with him. It is not easy to feel free before God. Not many people do. We all prefer in practice the security of the rules and the legality of the institutions as a refuge for our frailty and guarantee of pardon and grace. And we have full right to do so. But the day when God appears, even through the mists of the monsoon, and invites us to a greater closeness which entails leaving behind legal red tape and trusting each other in mutual openness, we have to answer the call, put aside all spiritual bureaucracy and live in freedom.

Breaking a mould, particularly a mould of many years and rich memories, is an event in a man's inner life, and has the effect of ushering in a new stage of spiritual development, since there is no question any more of passing from one mould to another, but of leaving the first and only one known till now, cutting off the dependence from something that seemed indispensable and is not so, and opening up to no fixed model but to a succession of them, or to a changing one, or to no model at all, to a non-model, as everything is possible when the monopoly of the former uniformity has been overcome. God can spring surprises on us if we are ready to allow ourselves to be surprised by him.

In India we say that no two monsoon are equal. Though the season keeps its appointment with cosmic regularity, as the stars in heaven and the tides in the sea; the beginning, the violence, the rhythm, the length, the parting of the four months are always different and make every rainy season individually unique and unforgettable. For me one of them was particularly so.

151

"The voice of the Lord echoes over the waters,
the Lord is over the mighty waters.
The voice of the Lord is power.
The voice of the Lord is majesty.
The voice of the Lord breaks the cedars,
the Lord splinters the cedars of Lebanon.
The Lord is king above the flood,
the Lord has taken his royal seat as king for ever.
The Lord will give strength to his people;
the Lord will bless his people with peace."

(Psalm 28)

THE PERFECT TRAVELLER

There are people who do not believe in God and deny his existence. Though while denying it they assert it in spite of themselves, since whoever opposes something, implicitly asserts the existence of what he opposes. "Militant atheism" is a profession of faith. Nobody fights a void. There are also people who sincerely declare not to know whether God exists or not, that is, they pose the question but do not find sufficient reasons to decide in favour of one answer or the other, and they accept their personal ignorance in genuine agnosticism. Finally, there are those who do not pose the problem, and simply prescind from the whole question in their thought and in their lives. Such is the line adopted by Buddhism; and I can speak about Buddhism too from India as family heritage, because it was here that is was born, and from here it has greatly influenced my own thought.

Buddha felt so much anguish before the problem of suffering, so much compassion for all living beings, that he could not stop to ask philosophical questions, much less to discuss them as the Brahmins did in those days of scholastic decadence, and against whom he sharply reacted. Buddha leaves theories aside and jumps into action. The key parable in his teaching is that of the wayfarer wounded by an arrow in the middle of the jungle. A group of travellers find him and begin to ask questions. Where did the arrow come from? Who shoot it? Why? What is its colour? What kind of wood is it made of? Till someone in the group senses the urgency and exclaims: But don't you see he is bleeding to death? Quick, stop the questions, take out the arrow, stanch the blood and bandage the wound so that he may live.

The wound, says Buddha, is the immoderate desire, the burning thirst described by the keenly Sanskrit word *trishana*, the anxiety to live and succeed and enjoy. Anxiety is a child of the future, is the unbalance between what we have and what we want to have, the hurry to have done today with the uncertainties of tomorrow. The solution is to tame that "tomorrow", and that is Buddha's aim. He does it with perfect logic within his system. Since he prescinds from God, Buddha defeats the future and plunges heart and soul into the present. That is Buddhism's greatest gift, the discovery of the present moment. No escape into the future or projection into infinity. No plans to carry out, and no worlds to redeem. Salvation is today, and heaven is here. Do what you do and be what you are from moment to moment. This is not denying the existence of a plan, a future, a hope ordered by the Supreme Being who rules the world; it is only prescinding from all that, and concentrating on life as it is at the instant I am living it. From there too comes the moral pragmatism Buddha expresses in his "middle way", far on one side from the austerities of Jainism which he himself practised in the beginning and gave up later, and on the other from the pursuit of pleasure that leads to frustration and suffering. Moderation in everything, which brings calm and peace in everything. Buddha is the

154

prophet of peace, and his images, to be found all over the East, and now throughout the world, irradiate and communicate that peace even today to whomsoever looks at them with the spirit with which they were made.

When I was studying theology in Poona which is close, by Indian standards, to the Buddhist "cathedrals" of Ajanta and Ellora, I asked my superior's permission to visit them, and I was refused. It was only many years later that I could get my own back, and I spent a whole day, solemn and recollected, in the greatest Buddhist sanctuary of all times. The unlikely location, the landscape in spontaneous semicircle, the immense caves, the repeated images, the smile captured in stone, the almost physical peace that enters all senses at once in an environment that is temple and nature and jungle and stone, made me live for a few consecrated hours the beneficent spirit of the prince turned prophet, and set on my soul the seal of their peace. There is one image of Buddha, before which I spent most of the time of my contemplative tourism, the memory of which still haunts me. Within the eternal stillness of its stone it seems to smile if looked at from the right side, to frown from the left side, and to bless in peace if looked at from the front. Sculptural skill and symbol of the immutability of the spirit in the midst of the vicissitudes of life, when the soul is at peace with itself, anchored in the present and firm in its acceptance of reality, while it acknowledges and reflects the passing shadows of the moods of the mind. There stands that rock, and there stands Ajanta in my memory and in the heart of India for ever.

In Ellora I saw the seminaries where the young Buddhist monks were trained. The bed, pillow, table and seat made out of stone, carved out of a single mountain, cell by cell as a huge and regular beehive in the rock; the board for daily notices also out of stone, the playgrounds, the central hall, the adjacent temple. There, before the granite strength of those eternal ruins, I understood the vital momentum that urged Buddhism on to the frontiers of India and beyond, and made of Shri Lanka, Burma, China and Japan permanent centres of Buddhism in all its branches. What I have never quite understood, and I think nobody really knows, for a number of contradictory explanations have been given, is why Buddhism disappeared from India. The monks left, the faith migrated, Hinduism reasserted itself and closed its ranks over the forgotten incident, which in India was a victory for the Brahmins, and in the whole world became a new essential chapter in the history of religion. That was the missionary expansion which took Buddhism all over the East, and made it part of Chinese wisdom and Japanese industry. And from there, already in our days, it has spread to the West where it has opened centres, multiplied literature and won favour in a wide sweep of peaceful conquest without equal in the history of human thought and religious ideas. Fifty years ago Buddhism in Europe was an antiquarian's oddity, known to a few and practised by none. Today the whole world has read Zen, has listened to a haiku and has seen karate. And all that is Buddhism.

I have read almost all the works of D. T. Suzuki, the quiet and humble professor who, most unassumingly and almost unawares to himself, decisively helped the spread of Buddhism in the West. With his shyness, his scholarship, his talks, his publications, his total lack of pretentiousness, proselytism or aggressiveness, he was the anonymous modern missionary who won for Buddhism in Europe and America in the twentieth century an acceptance similar to the one Francis Xavier obtained for Christianity in India and Japan

156

in the sixteenth, though with altogether different attitudes and methods. From among his books the one that has done me most good is "Zen and Japanese Culture", in which he shows, with tact and insight, how the whole of Japanese life, from the tea ceremony to a judo lock, is based on Zen. That is why I have just said that karate is Buddhism. And so are also the art of archery, fencing, origami, bonsai, ikebana, painting, gardening, management by consensus in business, the "No" theatre, all koan literature, monk stories and daily calligraphy.

I take this last example, though I begin my making it clear that I speak only from second hand, basing myself on some readings and a television programme on Chinese calligraphy. Maybe the fascination I experienced can make up for my ignorance in the matter. The rice paper, rough and absorbent, the thick ink that dries instantly, the broad and docile brush, and the wide sweeps in which hand, wrist and arm have full and open play... make corrections and erasures impossible, and that confers on Chinese writing its unique and significant character. Each stroke is the unique and unrepeatable result of a flying gesture. That is example and figure of the uniqueness of the present moment that has to be made use of in all its creative potential as it is now, without waiting to correct it in the future, because the opportunity will not be given. The ink dries up and the stroke lands on the paper once and for all in all its perfection... or all its clumsiness. When I type, as I am doing now, I have by my side on the table a rubber, correcting fluid with its diluent and white correcting tape to cover up, rub off, obliterate, correct and repeat from a single letter to a whole paragraph if necessary, and that is why I type distractedly, carelessly, with plenty of mistakes which afterwards I correct at leisure so that the final result is a neat page, rectangular, symmetrical, in parallel lines, all very practical and comfortable to read, but devoid of all art. Writing in the West, particularly now with electronic machines which allow correction before printing, is just a matter of producing black and white squares of very readable and very monotonous strokes; pure repetition of similar types, all very orderly... and very boring. In Chinese brush writing two characters are never equal, even if drawn by the same person, because each one is the result of the present moment in total concentration and spontaneous art, which express not only the meaning of the ideogram but the mood of the one who is drawing it with exclusive individuality at that moment. That is the cult of the present, the uniqueness of this instant, the commitment to reality and the full use of each successive moment in life, which makes of any performance a work of art, and of a written page a picture for an exhibition. That is the spirit of Buddism.

On the arch at the entrance of the Obaku temple in Kyoto (which I know only from a photograph) there is an inscription in large characters which is, they say, the main exhibit of the temple. The story goes that some two hundred years ago the sage Kosen drew it on paper, and from that model it was later carved in wood. His disciple, who was at the same time his critic, prepared gallons of ink and yards of paper, and greeted each attempt of the master with words like: "Badly done." "Very poor." "Even worse." After eighty-four attempts the disciple went out for a moment, and the master said to himself: "This is my chance!" Freed then from the distraction of the critical eye that wanted to ensure absolute perfection for posterity, he drew with bold spontaneity the decisive traits. The disciple-cum-critic came back and exclamed: "A masterpiece!" The inscription reads: "The First Principle."

158

I had always thought to myself and held before others that faith in God is the best and, in the last resort, the only real consolation and help in time of suffering. I may be suffering much right now, but I am sustained in my suffering by the thought that God loves me and looks after me, that he will not allow me to suffer beyond my strength, that he gives a redeeming value to my sufferings uniting them to those of Christ on the cross, and that with him he will take me to the glory of the resurrection where he will abundantly make up to me for all the present trials. Blessed be his name for ever. Precisely because of that conviction and security I had, I felt sorry for the atheist's condition who has no one to turn to when suffering strikes. This was so clear and evident to me that I was taken entirely by surprise at a passing reflection of Suzuki's who, in one of his innocent books with that neutral style of his, without even a hint of pressure or argument, or desire to convince anybody, stated simply the opposite conviction, namely that faith in God aggravates suffering, and it is harder for the believer to suffer than for the agnostic: "It is bad enough to suffer", he said, "but if on top of that we have to thank a loving God for sending us sufferings we do not understand, the tension may become unbearable." Almost like Psalm 55: "If my enemy were to curse me, I would put up with it; but if the affront comes from you, lifelong friend who used to sit at table with me...!" If my suffering came from a sworn enemy or a blind destiny, it would be bad enough, but after all such was to be expected and to be endured or counteracted manfully; but if the suffering comes from a provident God and loving Father who says he cares for me, who has the whole world in his hands and could certainly prevent my sufferings and does not do so for reasons known to him and unknown to me.., then I feel in myself the double tension of suffering the pain, and putting up with the unexplained attitude of a strange

159

God whom I, on top of it all, have to go on praising and thanking when I least feel like doing it. That can be very meritorious spiritually and very ruinous psychologically. There is no doubt that the East tolerates suffering much better than the West, and this may be one of the reasons for this true and verifiable fact. I am not abetting atheism, I am only exposing myself to other points of view, precisely because I have faith in my own, and letting them act on me to help me discover new directions for my own growth, new ways of understanding God and drawing close to him. For me it is clear that this reflection of Suzuki's, which I knew beforehand, read at random in one of his works the title of which I do not even remember because I had assimilated the idea without caring for the precise quotation, played a great part in my reaction to the monsoon which I have described in the previous chapter, because at that time I was precisely experiencing in myself the double tension he speaks about, the physical tension of the actual suffering (the rains in my case) and the moral tension of having to see God in it (my forced prayers), and I solved it in my own way with a closer and different intimacy with God within my own faith. If I am ignorant of other points or view, I cannot enrich my own.

The very word "Zen" is philologically Indian. It is only the adapted pronunciation, to Chinese lips first, *ch'an*, and then to Japanese lips, *zen*, of the Sanskrit word *dhyan* which means attention, concentration, meditation, contact in depth with the present moment; an idea which is basic in Indian Yoga, and from there passed on to Chinese Zen, giving it the very name it bears. Like many other Sanskrit terms, *dhyan* has been inherited by the modern Indian languages, and we use it freely every day without paying attention to its noble ancestry and its metaphysical reach. How many times in my mathematics class have I shouted to

160

an obviously distracted student that he had no *dhyan*, that he was paying no attention to what I was writing on the blackboard, that his mind was miles away from the classroom, and that, if he continued the way he did, he would be deprived of the wisdom of my scholarly explanations! When telling him that, I was preaching Zen without realizing it. That single word, *dhyan*, is the key of a healthy behaviour, of contact with reality, of mental balance, of the freedom of the spirit. Being what I am and doing what I do at every moment of day and life with committed zest and dedicated joy. That is Yoga and that is Zen. That is the way to solve problems in mathematics... and in life.

There was a modern Hindu saint in India who, while a young man at college, was reported to be very good at mathematics; there was no problem, particularly in geometry, that could resist the keenness of his intellect. Yet one day, so the story goes, he was distracted while tackling one such problem, got properly stuck, and could not concentrate sufficiently to see his way to a solution. Then he took a radical stand. He placed on his table an alarm clock set to ring an hour after the initial moment, and by its side he laid a naked knife, and declared, with the firm resolve for which he was well-known, that if the alarm sounded before he had solved the problem, he would take his own life. His companions watched intently in fear, but he now forgot everybody and everything around, achieved concentration and solved the problem. A similar story is repeated in Buddhism where an earnest monk, after many years and many efforts to achieve the liberation of the spirit, finally took an incense stick between his fingers, lit it and went into contemplation determined to attain illumination or burn his hand. They say that the instant the fire reached his skin was the blessed moment of his illumination. These are not

161

examples to be followed (if they happened at all), but parables on concentration, lessons on the intensity, the exaggeration of the present to hammer in with concrete blows the basic commandment to focus attention on what is happening now, never losing contact, but living out each moment in life simply by living it out, without being distracted with dreams of the future, spoling what I am doing now with the worrying thoughts of what I am going to do later. And this attitude is to hold in the daily business of earning a living as well as in the permanent business of earning eternal life. Both professional efficiency and traditional spirituality can draw great profit from the spirit of Zen.

The same principle is stated, in a striking paradox that cannot fail to shake the Western mind, by Lin-Yutang, whose works, from "The Empress Wu" to "The Wisdom of Laotze" passing through "The Importance of Living" I have read with profit and fruition. I smiled once in joy and surprise when I happened upon this unexpected Buddhist jewel in one of his writings: "The good traveller does not know where he is going; the perfect traveller does not know where he came from." I can hardly conceive an attitude that could be more opposed to my own attitude throughout life, my fixing objectives and choosing ideals, measuring efforts and calculating risks, studying tactics and selecting means, examining the past and planning the future, asking where I come from and answering in faith whither I am going; and yet when reading those words, almost from another planet, I feel my bones flower within me, I sense the most intimate core of my being vibrate with irresistible joy, I hear an echo that rises overwhelmingly from the bottom of my heart, a different call that invites me to explore other attitudes and travel other paths with the promise of adventure and thrill over unseen horizons, I realize that there is still much left for

162

me to learn and much to understand from the vast riches of wisdom and experience of mankind, and that I am lucky to know it and want it and launch out in unexpected caravan through the uncharted routes of unexplored thought. Each wandering is a poem and each step is a rhyme as my playful foot kisses the earth in fleeting love without stopping to calculate where the ballad is "going" or where life "leads to". The poem is beautiful and to be enjoyed by itself verse by verse, without having to wait for the last cadence in order to enjoy the first. The walk is valid in itself, and it takes up all its beauty when it is freed from the anxiety of arriving. Blessed ignorance of the future that gives back its full value to the present; blessed thoughtless (!) travelling that brings back the joy of wandering, the joy of living! I have struggled enough with my mind and my thought in my life, Lord, I have struggled enough! My whole life has been made up of plans and resolutions and efforts and promises and fights and battles against myself and my passions and the passions of the whole world struggling and striving for the final victory and the redemption of humankind. Allow me, please, for a while to forget it all and live for the sake of living, to enjoy the landscape, to feel my own breath, to hear my own steps, to walk in freedom upon earth. I want to be a Buddhist in the practical wisdom of living the totality of life in the intensity of each instant.

Jesus spoke in parables, and the Buddhist masters used the riddle, the puzzle, the conundrum, the paradox, the koan, the mondo that silence for a moment the logic of the mind to awaken from within it the intimate intuition of the spirit. I will allow myself just one Zen story. Three hermits lived together in a cave, and not a word passed between them. One day a wild horse in full gallop crossed the meadows before the cave, and the three hermits saw it.

163

Nobody, though, said anything. Three months later one of the hermits spoke and said: "That was a beautiful brown horse that passed through here the other day." Three months went by, and the second hermit spoke and said: "That horse was not brown, it was a bay." At the end of another three months it was the third hermit who spoke and said: "If you are going to be always quarrelling like this, I'll go away from here." Why does this silly story cause me such great delight, when at first sight it is no more than a modest joke or an absurd fantasy? I know that as soon as I ask "why?" I am out of Zen and I fall back into reasons and explanations, which is precisely what has to be avoided and suppressed to awaken the inner sense and let the light shine. But my mind is still active and wants to express itself.

I first of all take notice of the gaps induced in the dialogue. Three sentences that could be said in one minute take up nine months (which is precisely the time from conception to birth in man). That is making fun of old Father Time, and proving (not by syllogism but by a joke) that just as one minute can be extended to nine months, so can nine months be reduced to one minute (and the birth to a new life be instantaneous). The present can be made future (with cosmic results), and so can the future be made present in the real fun of ultimate enlightenment. Zen knows how to escape from the slavery of clock and calendar, to give back to the present moment its dignity and its value. Then there is in the story the lack of proportion between the slight disagreement between the first two hermits and the uncalled-for reaction of the third. It means that any quarrel in this world (and any problem at all for that matter) is always out of proportion, and that there is no reason to get angry or to take things seriously... not even the colour of galloping horse. And finally we have the horse itself, so

164

fleeting and swift that not even its colour can be perceived with certainty. The horse is the true self that gives only a passing glimpse and runs away to hide in the jungle of notions before we can ascertain its true colour. It is this fundamental point that justifies the breaking of silence on the part of the hermits and even their discussion. The true self is different from the apparent self limited by my body and my senses..., and with that we have arrived at the heart of Buddhism. The individual self of my memories, my faculties, my perceptions, the self locked up in the frontier of my skin and in the radius of my actions, is pure illusion. If there is no future, neither can there be a permanent substratum to hold and prolong my person from today to tomorrow, that is, there is no "I". The true self is the total reality, the universal conscience, the summing up of the whole actual reality reflected in me at this moment as the sea in a wave or the sun in a ray of light, without any attempt at defining matters more, as Zen itself wisely falls silent at this moment to make room for the unique dawn which is the quiet awakening of being in the centre of the soul.

This is the deeper sense of the parable of the wayfarer wounded by an arrow, with which I began this chapter. The arrow is the wrong idea of the self which has pierced our hearts as original conviction and constant source of all the evils we suffer in the painful smallness of this transitory and vulnerable existence. Pull out the arrow, come out of the narrowness and isolation of your meagre illusory identity, find your true self, and you will be free. Such was the enlightenment the Buddha received under the sacred tree in Bodh Gaya, and such was the way he immediately set out to preach in the Deer Park at Sarnath. I have also visited the park, and the deer still graze there.

165

GOD IS DIFFERENT

I quoted at the end of a chapter in this book Jesus' mysterious words: "Unless I go, the Holy Spirit will not come to you." Jesus is in no way an obstacle to the coming of the Holy Spirit, but the concept his disciples have of him, could be. Jesus had been for them such a concrete character and constant companion that his memory, his figure, his face, his voice limited and conditioned their way of understanding and finding God in their lives; and if now the Spirit has to come with a new experience, more intimate, subtle and overwhelming, they have to open themselves to a new idea of God, they have to transcend the only image to which they had clung so far. That is why Jesus has to go. It is he himself who is going to come back in the Spirit, but if he does not go in one form, he cannot come back in another. God has to go in order that God may come. That is the way the Church is built, and that is the way the Christian soul is formed in the greater knowledge of God and better understanding of divine things.

And now I dare to push forward this reasoning with Trinitarian logic, and to think that a moment comes in which the Holy Spirit, after filling up the soul with his gifts and regaling it with his intimacy as Jesus regaled his disciples with his own, says also with all the love of his presence and all the mystery of his divinity: "Unless I go, the Father will not come to you." If you always imagine God in the same way, however true and beautiful it may be, you will not be able to receive the gift of the new ways he had ready for you. And so the cycle continues, and the Father will also declare one day that he leaves in order that the Son may come again in a new understanding and a new birth. The mission of the divine Persons is to prepare us for new incarnations and new Pentecosts and new revelations; and the condition is always to leave God free to surpass one concept and offer another, to hide one face in order to reveal another, to go away one day in order to come back the next with a new facet of his infinite being. Unless God goes, God cannot come.

An important warning here. This process of coming and going, of leaving off and taking up, belongs to and is ruled by God, not by man. It is not for man to provoke change or experiment on his own with different "models" of the spirit, or, even more serious a matter, with one religion and another in order to be able to say that he knows all of them from the inside and so to gather information at his own risk. Some have done that, but to me that attitude appears presumptuous and irreverent. It is not for man to choose the way God has to come to him. On man's part the real attitude is reverence, eagerness, waiting, readiness to grasp a new hint, to be surprised, to change when God brings him the change, and to stay where he is, so long as he does not receive the invitation to move elsewhere. To appreciate what one has, to be open to what one can be given, and to be detached and prompt to answer the call when it comes.

168

To be on the alert. To live with the windows of the mind wide open: open for the Spirit to come in when he pleases..., and open for him to leave when he pleases. Always with the certainty that when he leaves, it is in order to come back with a new light and a new splendour.

If the change is not to be provoked, it is not to be feared either; on the contrary, it is to be desired and asked for, and we have to prepare ourselves positively for it with humility, generosity and courage, which are all needed in the always surprising adventure of the spirit. Our responsibility before spiritual change is double, embracing not only our own progress but also the advice and guidance and example we have to provide for others. On the one hand we have the welcome duty of knowing God better and drawing closer to him, which is the very meaning of our existence, the thrust of our longing and the goal of our efforts; and, on the other, we have the permanent charge to help others to understand God better, to enrich their prayer and to strengthen their faith. This leads us to know as many aspects of God as we can in order to be able to set before each person on each occasion the way that suits him best. God is the subject of our profession, and we have to know him well if we want to take him to all men.

I have said at the beginning of the book that in my own understanding and intention this book is a book against atheism, and I believe the idea must be clear by now. When the atheist rejects God, what he rejects is the image he has himself formed of God, and it is possible that if in due time he had known that there are other images, and he had accepted and lived them beforehand, he would not have come to this denial. It is easy to discard an idol one has oneself fashioned when the idol does not work any more. "I do not believe in the god in whom the atheists do not

169

believe" said pointedly patriarch Maximus IV in Vatican II. The best service we can render a man is to enlarge his concept of God for him. And, without reaching the point of atheism, I have watched many crisis of faith in the lives of religious men and women which sprung precisely from the concept of God they had lived with through life, and which, in a given trial and circumstances, had become too narrow for them, like clothes which, however beautiful and valuable, cease to fit when the person grows up: and so these persons were uncomfortable and uneasy within the narrow frame of the concept they had, unable to grow out of it because they did not have a larger one. Every crisis in faith is a crisis in the concept of God the person has at the moment, and so to enrich that concept is to strengthen his faith.

I once received a distressing letter from a far-off friend. The whole letter was a cry of pain at the death of his only daughter. She was a charming loving child who, with her arrival in this world, had changed her father's life filling it with light and with joy. I had played with her and shared in her father's love for that tender and transparent little being who seemed to have been made to spread happiness with her playful and mischievous presence. She had taken ill, the doctor was called for, nothing seemed serious, she had a sudden turn for the worse, and left for ever. The letter told his sorrow, and then went on to describe his own reaction. He had gone, he said, to the small altar he had in his house, before which he offered incense and prayers every morning with the new day, had taken the image that presided over the family gods and which all those days had been witness and object of his fervent prayers for his daughter's recovery, had lifted it violently in the air, and had smashed it against the floor into a thousand pieces. He had done to God, he said, what God had done to his child.

170

I respected his sorrow and his tears. I answered him as man to man and friend to friend. No rhetoric, no religious clichés, no formal attitude of God's official representative offering paternalistic condolences to a soul in pain. I only reflected his pain and expressed mine. And, as part of the sincerity I exacted from myself while writing to him, I exposed my conviction without discussing his, and gently added a sentence which opened the future without evading the present: "To me the image you have broken was not God's image, but the image of the god you had created for yourself. Maybe it has been broken because it had to break in order to make room one day for another image worthier of him." The advice, of course, had arrived too late, and the harm had been done: a broken image and a broken heart. But the lesson, if not for him certainly for me, remained sharp and urgent in my mind, and that is that we have to open up the idea of God in the minds of those who believe in him, so that they may believe better and save themselves in the inevitable crises that pain and suffering will bring into their lives. Many sacred ruins could have been avoided if the image had been renewed in time.

Thrice in this book I have used a phrase which I now use a fourth time as I draw to a close: we have to let God be God. That is the supreme act of worship, reverence and faith. To let him present himself as and when he wishes, to let him change, to let him evolve, to let him surprise us, to let him be whatever he wants to be, and to act in any way he wants to act; and if his behaviour does not fit within our frames, to be ready to change them, and never to reject his image simply because it does not meet our demands.

There was a celebrated slogan which opened Spain to international tourism years ago: "Spain is different." I cannot tell about Spain, but the phrase certainly fits God.

171

God is different. Not only is he different from everybody and everything else, but he is ever different from himself, and that is the very core of his divinity. God is different from God, since his infinitude brings always before man's limited understanding a new aspect, a new light, a new face, and it is that supreme freedom and variety that constitutes the essence of his being and the majesty of his presence. God is different, and we have to let him be so to his greater glory and our own profit. Everything is changing around us in our world, and full generations of genuine believers are clamouring for new ways to understand God and live their faith, just as religious men and women are asking for up-dated ways to understand their vows and live their consecration, and we have to provide them to save civilization and redeem humanity anew. And all this new understanding, vital and urgent, depends on our deeper understanding of God. The concept of God that each age brings out for itself is the key to its destiny. If we want to serve our times we can do no better than to find in our souls and proclaim in our lives a new fullness of the ever inexhaustible concept.

I end with the enlightening poem of an Indian friend, Karsandas Manek:

"Brother priest in God's holy temple... whoever you are,
open the windows of your temple
to let the breeze of the Spirit come through them,
to let the winds of grace blow through them,
to let God in through them.
Place on the altar the image you prefer,
recite your favourite prayers,
follow your traditional ritual;
but, please, leave open the windows of your soul
to let God in again."

172